The Haynes
Automotive
Detailing
Manual

by Jay D. Storer
and John H Haynes
Member of the Guild of Motoring Writers

The Haynes Automotive Detailing Manual
for cleaning and renewing cars and trucks,
inside and out

ABCDE
FGHIJ
KLMNO
PQRST

Haynes Publishing Group
Sparkford Nr Yeovil
Somerset BA22 7JJ England

Haynes North America, Inc
861 Lawrence Drive
Newbury Park
California 91320 USA

Acknowledgements

The authors are grateful for the help of many individuals and companies in the production of this book. We wish to thank Eagle One, One Grand Products, Wardlow Top Shop, and Performance Detailing for their cooperation and illustrations.

© **Haynes North America, Inc. 1994**

With permission from J.H. Haynes & Co. Ltd.

A book in the Haynes Automotive Repair Manual Series

Printed in the U.S.A.

ISBN 1 56392 113 8

Library of Congress Catalog Card Number 94-78660

While every attempt is made to ensure that the information in this manual is correct, no liability can be accepted by the authors or publishers for loss, damage or injury caused by any errors in, or omissions from, the information given.

94-192

Contents

1

Introduction

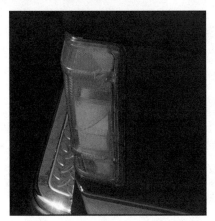

1 Introduction

Have you ever come across another example of the same car you drive? You're on the road or in a parking lot, and there's the exact duplicate of your car, same year, same model, same color, yet does the other car look brand new while yours is showing its age and mileage?

The difference between the two vehicles is the result of detailing, the technique of car care and visual enhancement that belies the reading on the odometer like a wrinkle cream for automobiles **(see illustrations)**. To some car owners, detailing means an occasional washing only after people start writing "wash me" in the dirt on the paint, while at the other end of the spectrum are the detailing aficionados, the owners of concours-restored specialty and classic cars. The latter group is in constant preparation for a white-glove inspection, waiting for a car show judge like he was a tough, marine-corps drill instructor ready to inspect the spotless bore of their service weapon.

1.1 It can be both frustrating and enlightening to run across a "twin" of your vehicle that seems to be in much better shape. It illustrates what yours could look like if you took care of it. These two pick-ups are the same model, same color, etc., but one looks like new and the other has faded, peeling paint and other signs of neglect.

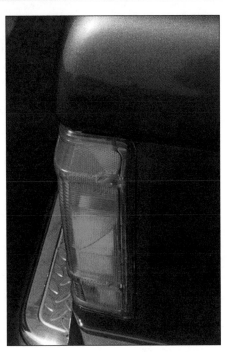

1.2 In closer detail, it's easy to see how much difference there is between "well-kept" and "unkempt". Here are examples of trim and paint on similar vehicles. Note the scrape marks on our neglected example - this should have been cleaned and retouched on a "detailed" vehicle.

The bulk of us are somewhere in between these two extremes. We don't truly neglect our vehicles, but we're always a little too busy to really go the extra mile in cleaning or detailing that could really make the difference. Seeing that "twin" of your own vehicle can really drive home the point of what your machine could look like if you had approached detailing properly, with the right products, the right tools and the right methods of application. That's where this book comes in. We're going to illustrate for you what can be done and how to do it right the first time.

We've taken tips and techniques our automotive-oriented staff has been using for years plus advice from some of the best pros in the detailing business and the leading companies making aftermarket car-care products to assemble a complete guide to car detailing. You probably won't follow every procedure we outline, or need to, but there is something here for everyone If you utilize just two or three of the "secrets" we'll reveal, you'll find them well worth the price of this book, just for those tips you needed.

Who needs a detailed car? If, when you saw that "twin" car, you felt a little embarrassed about the look of your own car in comparison, you're a candidate. The owner of that other car obviously took pride in his car's appearance, and with a little help from Haynes you can once again take pride in your ride. That is probably the main reason why most people are interested in the techniques of detailing, making their car look better.

Even an "economy car" can look good when it is nicely maintained, while a more expensive luxury car almost seems to require good detailing to maintain its image. It may be common to see a Hyundai or a Geo that's looking dirty or neglected, but rare to see a late-model Porsche, BMW, Jaguar or Corvette in the same state. The bottom line is that good detailing, or car "grooming" if you will, improves the image of any vehicle and shows a certain pride taken by the owner. They say that clothes make the man, and even a person of modest budget can

1.3 In some vehicle details, such as these stainless-steel shelled rear-view mirrors, the neglected part can be "revived" with proper detailing for an appearance almost as good as new. Other areas, like paint and exterior rubber, may not be so easily restored when long neglected.

look good with a good haircut and clothes that are clean and neatly pressed. You don't have to wear an Armani suit to take pride in your appearance. Ever driven in a neighborhood where the majority of houses seem unkempt or little cared for? You'll always find a few streets where the yards are beautifully-kept; there's a nice little white fence out front, and the houses are neatly painted and trimmed. That's detailing of real estate, and the procedures can make your vehicle stand out as much as those houses do in a sea of surrounding houses that exhibit no pride.

Protecting your investment

Some might say, "Well, a house is an investment and needs to be spruced up to maintain its value, while a car is merely transportation." Anyone who says that hasn't been shopping for a car lately! In the last 20 years, the average new-car price has increased almost ten-fold. For example, a new Ford Mustang could have been purchased in 1965 for under $2500; today the same new Mustang would cost many times that amount.

It is commonly said in financing circles that "buying a new car is the second-largest purchase an individual is likely to make in his or her lifetime (the first being a house)." Not only is this true, but for many older buyers in today's new-car market the price of a Cadillac or even a Ford could be more than they paid for their house 20 years ago! That can come as quite a shock, but it points out the truth that today a vehicle is just as much of an investment as a house, and in the same need of detailing and maintenance to protect that investment.

That's the second-biggest reason people are interested in detailing, for the economic benefits. If you've just laid out 20-30 thousand for a new car, and we're not even talking about the sports or luxury models, you're concerned about keeping it looking good so that it maintains its best value until you're ready to either sell it or trade it in on your next vehicle. Granted, most cars will maintain their looks pretty well with minimal care in the first two or three years, but after that the age will eventually tell without good maintenance. Unfortunately, most of us have four or five-year financing on a new car today, and our investment needs to be protected well enough so that it still looks good when we make that satisfying last payment.

Those people who trade in their new car every year or two can probably get by with nothing more that standard washing and waxing, but cars kept longer

1.4 Hard to believe, but this Mercedes was 12 years old when the photo was taken, yet it looks as good or better than new. It belongs to a professional detailer who managed to buy it "right," detail it thoroughly and then maintain that level of appearance. A well-maintained car like this will always be salable at the high end of the "blue book."

1.5 Just as mechanics like to buy used cars that need mechanical work, you may be able to buy a used car that is very sound mechanically and low in mileage yet has been neglected in terms of detailing. Three or four weekends of your labors on a faded yet sound paint job and you'll have a nice used car for less than any dealer would charge.

than that require a more thoughtful approach. Most owners today keep their cars for at least four or five years, and may even let them "trickle-down" within the family, keeping them for enough years to pass them along to a son or daughter when the family gets a new car. Your children will thank you for having kept good detailing on that handed-down car, and your pride in ownership will have been a good role model for your children. They will have learned to respect and care for their own vehicles over the years **(see illustration)**.

What about used cars? This is where detailing really pays off. In fact, the traditional American used-car lot has always been the place where detailing was a closely-guarded secret "art" practiced by the "wizards" out back who could make a rental car look like it had been owned and maintained by the proverbial "little old lady who only drove it on Sundays to church" **(see illustration)**. If you're ever in a position to trade in a car at a dealership, keep an eye on their used-car lot for a few weeks after your trade-in. You may be surprised to see your old car in their lot, looking very nice indeed, and for sale for quite a bit more than they gave you as a trade-in allowance! That's how used-car operations make considerable money. They buy cars at wholesale auctions, detail them vigorously and put them out on their lot for a considerable profit margin. They have probably steam-cleaned the undercarriage so that no fluid leaks are evident, cleaned and detailed the engine until it looks like it has always been maintained by a fastidious, engineer-type owner, cleaned the carpets and interior, maybe put in a set of floormats and a trunk mat, buffed the original paint to a fare-thee-well and maybe even put on a set of inexpensive but brand-new tires which just happen to disguise any chassis or alignment problems the vehicle may have. We're not saying that such dealers are doing anything dishonest here (no mention of speedometer turn-backs, which we hope are less common than they used to be), simply that they are in the business of making cars look better when they sell them than when they bought them. The difference is strictly in the detailing.

If you want to see how detailing can improve a vehicle's appearance and apparent age, just visit a few used-car operations and open a few doors, hoods and trunks **(see illustration)**. Keep in mind that these cars didn't come into the dealer looking that clean - detailing was involved. Anything the dealers have done, you can do yourself and, with the help of this book, probably do it better. Let's say you have a used car that you're about to sell. You've been to a few dealers

1.6 A good used-car lot is the perfect place to see the fruits of detailing labor. Most quality lots will buy cars wholesale and send them to a pro detailing shop for a "makeover." Ever wonder why there never seem to be any high-mileage-looking cars in the used-car lot?

1.7 A good looking car on the used car lot has had the full treatment, including paint buffing and waxing, glass cleaning, tire and wheel detailing, engine cleaning and full interior cleaning. The dealer will realize much more than the cost of the detailing work in added sales value of the detailed vehicle.

and they aren't willing to give you what you want in trade. Now you're considering a private-party sale, via some ads in the newspaper, to get a higher price. Here's where the advice we have can pay off. A weekend spent detailing your old car can mean the difference between getting "low book" and getting top dollar. It's the perfect way to show your car in its best light to prospective buyers and can reward you handsomely for your labors.

Save on buying a used car

The detailing edge is also helpful when you are shopping for a used car to buy. If you consistently shop private-party cars via the classifieds rather than at used-car dealers, you have noticed that not everyone knows about detailing. You're looking for a specific make, model and year, and within those parameters you'll find both creampuffs and lemons for sale. Try to find the car you want that is mechanically sound, relatively-low in mileage but which doesn't look like it just came off the showroom floor. A sound paint job that is just dirty or faded, combined with dirty floor mats and marked-up bumpers can knock a considerable amount off the apparent value, allowing you to get a good car for a good price, knowing that you can detail it later **(see illustration)**.

Mechanics often shop for good-looking used cars that have mechanical problems. Since the mechanic has all the tools and abilities to fix the mechanical problems, he winds up with a good overall car for a reasonable investment. Many are the mechanics and bodymen who turn "fixer-upper" used cars into a profitable sideline. Most of us don't have the knowledge or equipment for advanced bodywork or mechanical repairs, but detailing is something everyone can do. Thus, we look for a used car that is mechanically good but a "fixer-upper" in the looks department.

Let us not mislead you; taking a neglected vehicle and making it show-worthy is no easy task. There's more involved in a good detailing job than just washing and waxing. If you're just prepping an old car for a quick sale, you won't be following all of the chapters of this book in detail, but if you do want to keep a car and maintain it at its best the detailing doesn't need to be done all at once.

There will be an initial investment of time and a few dollars, but, once the

1.8 If you have overspray, a severely-faded paint job or some other detailing problem that requires professional buffing, the pro detail shop is your next stop. They can give you professional advice on how to take care of your vehicle, and they are one of the few sources where you can get engine and chassis steam-cleaning done.

main areas of detailing have been addressed with some elbow grease, the rest of the details can be handled one at a time, say one item per weekend, until it's all done. Once fully detailed, you'll find that good appearance is simply a matter of maintenance after that, and a car prepared properly is actually very easy to keep looking its best.

Professional detailing

As mentioned above, detailing used to be a secretive art practiced only at the used-car dealership and a few professional detail shops. The latter places of business were always low-profile ventures whose main clientele included dealerships that farmed out their detailing and car enthusiasts who were "in the know." They may have been associated with large car-wash operations where the detailing operation became an outgrowth of their steam-cleaning bay. After steam-cleaning engines for dealers, fleet operators and automotive shops, it was only natural that the carwash would eventually be asked to repaint an air cleaner and pair of valve covers, and perhaps wipe down all the wires and hoses with a rubber rejuvenator. Someone on the staff eventually got known as a "detailer."

There are professional detail shops still today, although not as low-profile and hard-to-find as they once were **(see illustration)**. In the author's town of about 85,000 population, the Yellow Pages of the phone book have a heading for Automobile Detailing with some 32 companies listed. Of these, some are part of large carwash operations, most are separate shops and about one-third are the relatively-new phenomenon of mobile detailing businesses.

These latter businesses have become quite popular, at least in Southern California, in the last five years or so, with the general availability of portable equipment. The typical mobile-detail outfit consists of a mini-truck towing a utility-size trailer which carries a 100-200-gallon water tank, 5-horsepower gas-powered generator, 5-horsepower pressure-washer and an industrial vacuum. The mini-truck is usually fitted with a shell and carries all the cleaning and detailing supplies. Some are operated with only one person, but many have two people **(see illustrations)**.

1.9 Mobile detailing, with a truck, trailer and two people can be an excellent business for those who like to work outdoors and be independent. In the last ten years, mobile detailing has become more popular, especially with customers who don't have time to do it themselves or who don't trust their car "investment" to a standard, brush-type, carwash.

1.10 Once you start getting into detailing your own vehicle, you will be making a number of buying trips to the local auto parts or chain store for the supplies. You'll likely be greeted by an overwhelming array of products. Reading this book should give you a much better sense of which products you really need.

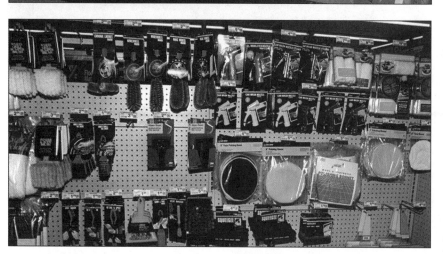

1.11 If you are a car "enthusiast" and travel to various car events in your area, you will probably find several booths of detailing supplies for sale. Wherever collector car owners are gathered, the subject of which wax to use is always a topic.

1.12 Auto parts stores also carry a wide array of detailing tools and related equipment.

1.13 The extensiveness of the paint cleaning/protection line is one aspect that distinguishes the "pro" products from the waxes advertised heavily on television. The "consumer" products combine functions and try to make everything seem easy (the "five-minute, no buffing" car-cleaning system), while the pro line has varying grades of polishes, glazes and compounds, each with its own specific purpose.

1.14 Even if your vehicle has been neglected in the past, application of the advice in this book can put you back on track toward a vehicle that looks great inside and out. The psychological aspect is that, once the hard work is done, you will take much more pride in your vehicle, get compliments on it, and sometimes it almost seems like the detailed vehicle even runs better.

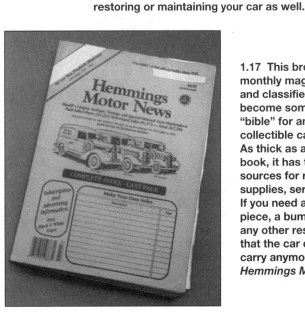

1.15 Where you can really see true attention to detailing is at car events where many similar vehicles are judged in concourse competition. If you get to the even early enough, you can see how the owners of restored vehicles detail their cars for the show, and they may share advice on restoring or maintaining your car as well.

1.16 Not only does a well-detailed car "feel better" when driving, it is also easier to maintain mechanically. It's a pleasure to check the oil on a clean engine, and, when kept clean, any leaks that indicate potential problems can be addressed right away, before things get expensive.

1.17 This brown-covered monthly magazine of display and classified ads has become something of the "bible" for antique and collectible car enthusiasts. As thick as a small phone book, it has thousands of sources for restoration supplies, services and parts. If you need an interior trim piece, a bumper bracket or any other restoration part that the car dealer doesn't carry anymore, it'll be in *Hemmings Motor News.*

1.18 A mail-order source of high-end automotive tools and quality detailing products is Griot's Garage (see Sourcelist for address).

1.19 The older a vehicle gets, the more apparent good detailing becomes. You can keep a brand-new car looking good for perhaps three years with little effort, but, after that, only the detailed car is going to continue to look good. When you have an older collectible car like this one, great paint, interior and engine will always draw admirers.

1.20 The engine compartment of the same car shows the level of pride taken in all aspects of the vehicle's appearance. This has been restored to better-than-new, with everything shinier and neater than showroom and not a speck of dirt to be seen.

1.21 Car enhancements are sold almost universally, while some truck accessories can be more difficult to find. A good first source is the local camper-shell dealer who often carries a lot more than just campers.

Mobile detailers can travel anywhere to clean just about any kind of vehicle, from a sports car to a motorhome, a pick-up to an 18-wheeler. Some of their clientele are business customers; others are private parties. The typical customer is either someone who doesn't trust their expensive car to a commercial car wash or a busy middle-income working person who doesn't have time to get to a car wash. Regardless, all appreciate the convenience of having the detailers come to their homes or businesses to perform the work. While the detailers are hard at work in the parking lot, the car owner never has to leave his office. Many busy people schedule regular appointments for detailing, as they would for a

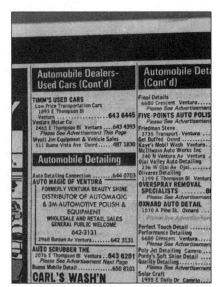

1.23 Mobile detailing rigs travel to your home or business; you don't even have to leave your chair. Because they are self-contained, they don't require any electricity or water connections and thus can operate anywhere: at a truck stop, parking lot, remote ranch or even an oil rig.

1.22 Your local Yellow Pages may have a separate category for "Automobile Detailing". These are the places to look for when searching for special detailing services and pro supplies. Many detail shops buy professional materials in large quantities, and they may sell you a small quantity of a product not otherwise available in stores.

1.24 Mobile detailing can be done with just one operator, but he must be fleet of foot and with a great sense of what detail or section to do and in what order. Most operations have two people working together for quicker work and less chance of any area drying out or spotting before the detailer gets to it.

1.25 Trailer-mounted detailing rigs can be simple or elaborate. This is typical of many, with toolbox, water tank, generator and pressure-washer.

1.27 This 5hp generator is generally used most for powering an industrial wet/dry vacuum cleaner but could also be used to run a buffer or any other power tool that may be needed in the field.

1.26 For those interested in detailing professionally, this 5hp pressure-washer is perfect for most jobs. Such gasoline-powered equipment should last a long time with good maintenance because on each job they are operated only a short time.

haircut or other service, but these mobile detailers do make house calls!

The 100-gallon water tank can wash at least ten cars, so to do more in one spot you'll need to refill or use that company's outside hose connections. The mobile detailing business has been around about ten years but has grown rapidly (at least on the West Coast) in the last three years or so. If you start getting really interested in detailing as a business, this is one of those trends we can see spreading to the rest of the country, and you could have the business to yourself if you start one in your area.

There is even a Professional Detailers Association, whose address is in the Sourcelist at the back of this book. The national organization has around 400 members, with the biggest chapter being in Southern California where lots of automotive trends originate and where the automobile as an obsession or way of life is a well known cliché, but a great one!. Of the 90 members in the Southern California chapter, the majority are operators of mobile detailing rigs. Detailers have always been somewhat secretive and kept their arcane "tricks" close to the vest. But the PDA has been around now for four or five years, and many are starting to come around to sharing with their fellow detailers. The aim of the organization is to aid in cross-training, spread helpful information and raise the level of professionalism in the business. There has even been some talk of eventual certification programs. There are several trade magazines that deal with the detailing business: *Professional Carwash and Detail*, *American Clean Car* and *Auto Laundry*, all of whose addresses are in our Sourcelist at the end of the book.

Detailing prices at stationary detailing shops are about the same as with the mobile operations. You will most likely have to leave your car there, which is less convenient than the mobile operations, but some additional services can be done in a shop that can't be done in a parking lot, such as paint repair, undercoating, true steam-cleaning of engines and chassis and buffing/restoration work on oxidized and old paint. You generally find experienced, knowledgeable personnel at detailing shops, and, in later chapters of this book, you'll see some of them in action giving you the benefit of tips they have learned over the years.

One final word about the definition of "detailing." To true car afficionados, it means more than simply cleaning a vehicle for best appearance. The word detailing to them also implies a sense of style. When you use Ty-wraps to straighten out a jumble of underhood hoses or wires, paint your metal windshield-wiper arms flat black, install aftermarket wheels or hubcaps or opt for a set of chromed

1.28 If you have a rare specialty vehicle like this Lamborghini LM-002, you can't trust it to a standard carwash, and establishing a good relationship with a mobile detailer for regular, consistent car care is the best way to protect a considerable investment.

valve covers and a shiny new air cleaner housing, you are applying the style element of detailing. It's a subjective thing since what looks good to one person may not appeal to the next, but many car enthusiasts include accessorization, personalization and mild customizing as part of the world of detailing. The person applying the term may be a Lexus owner who pays extra to get gold-plated trim on his car, to a 4x4 driver who wants a chromed differential cover, but the attitude is the same. "I want my vehicle to stand out, and to say something about me as a person." That's the true essence of detailing.

Notes

Body exterior

2

2 Body exterior

Most people assume that they know all there is to know about washing and waxing their cars. How difficult can it be? After all, according to the television ads for the widely known brands of polishes, you can make your car look like a showcar (and thus attract beautiful models as are seen around their cars) in about five minutes' time with no effort required. We hate to let you down, but your parents were right when they said "nothing good comes easy," and that certainly applies to detailing an automobile.

2.1 Achieving good, clean shiny paint is probably the single most important aspect of detailing. The outside of the car is what is seen most, and paint covers 90% of the exterior. Once you achieve a good detailing "baseline" on your paint, future cleaning will be relatively simple, and you'll take continued pride in your vehicle's appearance. In a sense, detailing is like keeping up a physical regimen at a gym: once you start neglecting matters it can be hard to get back to the baseline goal.

Even for a brand new car, proper preparation for taking care of the finish will involve some elbow grease on a regular basis. On a car even a year old that hasn't been meticulously maintained, some definite effort is necessary at the start. What you are trying to do is establish what we'll call a detailing "baseline." Once the effort has been invested to bring your vehicle to that baseline, only regular maintenance will be required thereafter.

The important factor is obtaining a paint job that is clean, undamaged, and glossy and then protecting that finish with a good wax. When you've achieved that attractive baseline the rest is easy, and how hard it is to get there depends strictly on the condition of your existing paint.

There are a lot of factors that negatively impact your car's exterior, including, of course, sun and weather but also industrial pollution and natural disasters (for your paint at least) like tree sap, pollen, bird droppings, bug splatters, spots from hard water and maybe the neighbor's cat who likes to curl up on your warm hood once in a while and

2.2 Many cars today feature basecoat/clearcoat paint finishes. A little bit of neglect can have more serious consequences here than on conventional paints. Once a section of the clearcoat has deteriorated, particularly on metallic paints as shown here, no amount of buffing or waxing will restore the area to like-new condition.

isn't overly concerned about the impact of his clawed little feet on your pride and joy. Industrial pollution in the air attacks paint, rubber, plastic and chrome, whether they're on a Rolls-Royce or a Subaru. Perhaps the most insidious pollutant is the acid rain we get. What nature intended to be the purest water comes down to us carrying all sorts of airborne particles and chemicals. In most areas of the "snowbelt," both sand and corrosive salts are used on the roads in the winter. Sand and salt don't just dull your paint job; they eat away the steel itself underneath!

Unfortunately, there is no miracle cure for paint protection, just good pro-

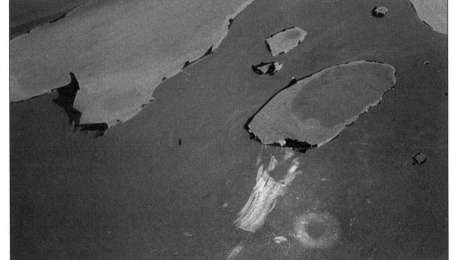

tectants applied regularly with equal parts elbow grease and common sense. Most of us have seen "infomercials" on the TV channels for miracle waxes or heard a new-car salesman's pitch about the "Teflon-coating" they are offering as an option with your new car. You can believe such stories if you like, but don't ever mention it to a professional detailer. He's either going to laugh or get angry! The fact is, if detailing were that easy the pros wouldn't be in business long.

2.3 Some of the earlier vehicles with clearcoated metallic paints actually had factory-defective clearcoats that lasted only two years, after which the unprotected basecoats could actually blister up and peel off, especially on hoods where there is engine heat from below as well as exterior UV rays and heat from above.

Washing basics

Every detailer will tell you the most common mistake made by average motorists in cleaning their cars is the soap they use. Never use common household cleaners, whether laundry soaps, dish soaps or even hand soaps to wash your car! There are some household products that have a place in some areas of detailing, but washing isn't one of those areas. Household soaps are much too strong for your paint finish, rubber or chrome, and can dull paint and leave light-colored streaks. Always wash with specific car-washing soaps. These can be

2.4 A well-stocked automotive supply store will have an array of car-care chemicals, from washes to waxes, glass cleaners, vinyl protectants, whitewall cleaners, tire blackeners and interior cleaning/protection products.

2.5 You won't need a trunkful of chemical products to detail your car. A basic kit would include a good wash soap, polish, wax and a vinyl protectant. You can use a variety of brands, finding out what works best for you, but most enthusiasts and detailers stick with one "line" of supplies for the sake of compatibility.

2.6 A typical store will have a good line of applicators, towels, sponges, wash mitts and related car-washing products in addition to all the chemicals.

2.7 It's important to wash and rinse a section of your car at a time, and in the shade, to prevent water spots like these from forming on your paint. In areas where there is high mineral content in the water supply ("hard" water), such water spots can actually eat into the paint and cause minute craters if they aren't removed right away.

purchased in any auto supply store or discount chain store. They clean your car gently and can be purchased in quantity sizes that make them economical to use as well.

The second most common mistake is washing the car outside on a sunny day. Even in areas where the tap water isn't particularly hard, you will get unsightly, hard-to-remove water spots all over the paint job when your wash water dries "instantly" on the hot sheetmetal, chrome and glass. In areas of the country where water is hard (i.e. high mineral content), these water spots can be very difficult to remove and may require abrasive paint cleaners which you don't want to use if you can help it.

2.8 A large, soft sponge can be used to wash your vehicle, but detailers prefer to use a sheepskin "mitt." They are soft, have essentially two sides to work with and will absorb and disperse a lot of soapy water, which means less trips back and forth to the wash bucket.

2.9 Some sheepskin wash aids aren't mitts at all, having no hand hole inside. This large one holds a considerable amount of soapy water. Anything the pros can do to save time and still do a good job is considered a worthwhile detailing-tool investment.

Wash your vehicle indoors, if possible, or at least in cool shade, and cool the car off with a good rinsing before you begin to wash. Usually, the wheels and tires are washed last; then the body of the car is washed from the top down. Use only true car-washing soap in a bucket of warm water (not hot, not cold), and put a strong spray of water into the bucket when filling to generate lots of suds. The foamy suds help to reduce surface abrasion during washing, by keeping the surface "lubricated" at all times. Apply the soapy solution with a large, soft car-washing sponge or, better, a car-washing mitt **(see illustration)**.

If your vehicle is particularly dirty around the bottom from traveling through puddles or mud, use your hose nozzle to direct a really strong spray of water on the dirty areas such as the fenderwells, tires/wheels, bumpers, front spoiler and rocker panels. You should be able to dislodge the majority of heavy deposits. What you must not do at any time is drag big dirt deposits around on your wash mitt. The dirt can scratch the rest of the painted areas where you use the mitt. Naturally, the mitt needs to be rinsed out frequently, in a separate bucket of water. Do not put the dirty mitt back into your clean solution of soapy water. The bucket you use for rinsing the mitt should be emptied and refilled when the water gets dirty, which may be several times during a car wash if the vehicle is particularly dirty. A mud-encrusted four-wheel-drive should be cleaned with a high-pressure nozzle at a coin-op car wash before you bring it home to detail. Use the wash "wand" to get up underneath everywhere, even behind the bumpers, suspension, frame and crossmembers. Any place where dirt is allowed to accumulate can collect water later on and rust will be sure to follow.

Back to our home wash-up, you are starting with the roof, hood and trunk lid, then working your way down the sides, followed by front end and rear end. Do not use hard hand pressure on your wash mitt. If there are really stubborn spots or stains, you can take care of them later with the proper product, but during the wash phase you don't want to use the mitt as if it were a buffer; this will drag dirt around and scratch the paint.

Once you have the car clean, it's time to rinse it off. You must make sure to get any soapy water solution off of the finish as quickly as possible. Even the

2.10 When you first rinse your car to cool the surface off before starting to wash and wax it, you will notice how shiny it looks with a sheet of water on the surface. We'd all like our car to look that good when we're done, but such a reflective surface isn't achieved without lots of elbow grease, at least at first.

2.11 When water rinses off the sides of your car like this, in sheets, it's obvious that the surface has no wax protection and it's time for a full detailing of the exterior.

specialized car-washing soaps can have a dulling effect on paint if left to dry on the finish. Also, the soaps dry with a slightly sticky surface, and any place on your car left sticky will become a dirt magnet. Use common sense. The areas that are hardest to clean will also wind up being the areas where dirt and moisture can collect over time to create paint or chrome problems, even body rust. So when rinsing, be thorough.

While a strong spray from your garden hose nozzle was helpful at the beginning to loosen dirt, now that you are rinsing you want to use the hose without a nozzle. Detailers say that the next phase, drying the car, can be performed a lot quicker if you get more water off the surface. They use a low-pressure flow from the hose, held close to the car, to "flood" areas of the sheetmetal **(see illustration)**. Try this! It makes the water come off in sheets, leaving much less water on the car's surface. When you use a hard spray to rinse the car, the overspray keeps getting on other areas of the car, and you never get all of it off, so consequently you use a lot of towels for drying.

Another pro's tip for drying the car is to use a squeegee but *not* the kind that have a windshield-wiper-type rubber. Those would be much too hard for your paint job. There are drying squeegees made with a soft rubber which work great at getting large flat areas of glass and sheetmetal clear of

2.12 Your auto accessory store or large chain merchandiser will have an array like this of buckets, hose attachments, brushes and even long-handled brush-tipped hose washers for cleaning tall trucks and RVs.

2.13 The most common car-care mistake is using the wrong kind of soap. Each product has its own uses, but the function with each type is to help fill in the minute valleys of your paint finish. Instead of strong household soaps, use dedicated carwashing soaps, of which you'll find an ample array available at your auto supply store.

2.14 Before beginning your wash operation, look the vehicle over for stubborn spots like bird droppings, tree sap, bug splatters and tar deposits. Tar and bug deposits can be removed with commercial products just for this purpose. Do these spots first; then your washing will remove any residues left from such cleaners.

2.15 Road tar deposits can be removed easily and safely with household kerosene lamp fluid. It's basically just scented kerosene and doesn't leave your hands or rags smelling like straight kerosene.

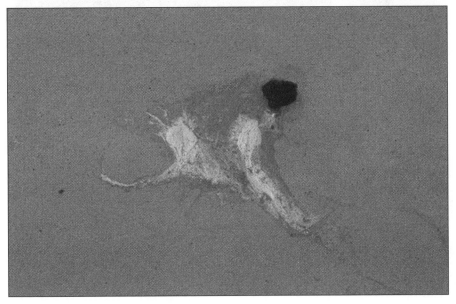

2.16 Don't wait for your regularly scheduled car-washing to take care of bird splatters like this. The bird stuff can eat into your paint if left too long. When you see such a deposit, soften it first with a spritz of water, let that soak, then take the mess off with a paper towel. When dry, follow with a local application of a cleaner-wax or "five-minute detailer" product to ensure the paint is clean.

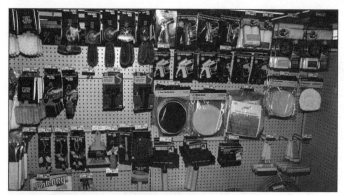

2.17 A good, non-kinking hose and a hose nozzle are basic tools you'll need for any home detailing. This store display also features squeegees and buffing pads.

2.18 For a good "driveway" wash and detail, you should have two clean plastic buckets, one with soapy water and the other just plain water for rinsing your wash mitt. Fill the wash bucket by adding a few ounces of car-washing soap, then use your hose nozzle to fill with water, making lots of suds.

2.19 The bucket of clear water is for rinsing the wash mitt only. After washing an area of the car, do not put the dirty mitt back in the sudsy bucket without first rinsing it out in the clear bucket. On a 4WD or other dirty vehicle, you may have to change the rinse water several times during the car wash.

2.20 Wash just one section of the car at a time. Start with the roof and the windows, then the hood, grille and front fenders as the next section, followed by the rear and the sides. Do the tires and wheels last. The reason for doing a section at a time is to get to the rinse phase on each section before the suds and loosened dirt have a chance to dry onto the surface.

2.21 Don't forget to wash the door jambs, interior edges of the trunk lid and the bottom of the hood, as they are difficult to clean later. Door jambs are best rinsed with a clean sponge and water, rather than with a hose which can get water spray on the interior.

2.22 Many pro detailers rinse a car by removing the spray nozzle and just flushing the surface with a large volume of water rather than a hard spray. There's less contamination of the other sections, and the surfaces dry quicker with less spotting.

2.23 A squeegee with a very soft rubber edge can be used to slide rinse water off large flat areas of sheetmetal. This saves on towels and chamois-wringing when it comes to drying off the surface. (photo courtesy Eagle One).

90% of the water.

Now you start in with either a natural or artificial chamois. There actually is an animal called the chamois, described in the dictionary as "a small, goatlike antelope of Europe and the Caucasus," and the secondary definition is a "soft pliant leather made from the skin of the chamois or sheepskin. We would call a natural chamois for car drying one made from "some kind of" animal. They have been used for as long as there have been automobiles, with some of the best natural chamois coming from Great Britain **(see illustration)**. They are as soft as a baby's skin when you first buy them, but once used for drying water off your car they dry up into something like the stiffness of cardboard. Once you wet it again in warm water, it comes back to "life" and is soft once more. They work like a very fine version of a sponge, absorbing water from paint, glass and chrome, without either abrading the surface (like a true sponge would do when it is unlubricated by soap) or leaving any streaks behind. The latter benefit makes a chamois the perfect tool for drying glass.

A chamois must be taken care of properly. Good natural chamois are expensive but will last for years if cared for. Clean them in warm, soapy water; then rinse the soap out of them with clear water. Never put the chamois away dirty or store in a closed container when wet. Even fine dirt particles embedded into a chamois can cause minute scratches in your paint. Chamois manufacturers recommend cleaning with mild soap flakes, not harsh detergents that will remove the natural oils. Your chamois will accumulate some darker areas after use. This is from hitting the black rubber trim on the car while drying the body. Such staining is inevitable and doesn't diminish the ability of the chamois to work as intended.

In recent years, artificial chamois have become widely available. They consist of man-made materials, making them less ex-

2.24 Natural chamois is still the traditional tool for drying off paint, chrome and glass. A chamois absorbs a lot of water, can't scratch the surfaces (if the chamois is kept clean) and doesn't leave streaks on the surfaces. The larger the chamois, the more expensive it is, but a good one will last for many years.

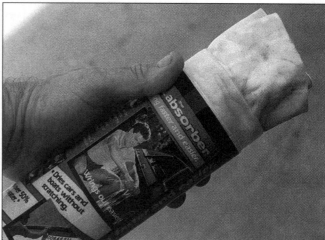

2.26 Natural chamois will dry up and harden after use and will have to be softened with clean water before the next use, but the artificial ones don't attract mildew and can be stored slightly damp in their original airtight containers so they can be ready anytime.

2.25 Artificial chamois also work very well at absorbing large amounts of water, thus drying a surface quickly to prevent water spots. Drag it flat across a large area, wring it out, and then go back with it wadded up to remove any remaining water.

2.27 Many detailers use only clean cotton toweling for drying cars , feeling they are better able to get into nooks and crevices than with a chamois, and they save time by not having to constantly wring out a chamois. They use small towels and use lots of them, so they usually have a commercial laundry service supply them.

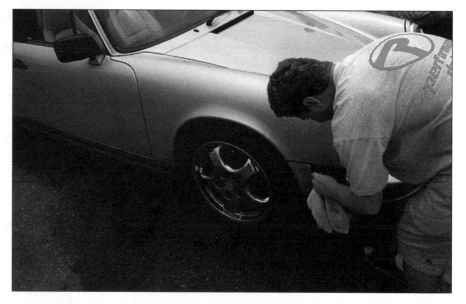

pensive, and they can absorb a lot more water than a natural chamois because they can be manufactured thicker **(see illustration)**. Many of these artificial chamois are hawked (and demonstrated) by slick salesmen at swap meets, car shows and other venues. You can buy them at prices ranging from a few dollars to as much as $20. We recommend that you spend a little more and get a quality one in your local auto parts or chain store. You're looking for one that emulates the very smooth appearance of a real chamois. The artificial ones on which you can actually see the pores may absorb a lot of water, but they may also scratch your paint.

A car can be dried completely with chamois, but there will be a lot of wrist-bending wringing-out when you get down to the last beads of water. Most pros use terrycloth towels for final drying. Such towels should be 100% cotton, and you should buy and set aside towels just for the drying phase of your detailing. Never use a towel for other aspects of detailing, such as waxing, polishing or

2.28 According to the pros, there are chemical product lines which are better for the serious detailer than the typical, heavily-advertised brands but much more widely available than the commercial "pro" products they use. A good indication of a quality line are paint and wheel care products with varying stages of aggressiveness and complete compatibility among their own products.

2.29 The One Grand line of vehicle care products has been around since 1933, mostly serving the detailing professionals and owners of specialty show cars. Some paint and detail shops sell the line as well as use it, and they can be purchased by mail in consumer-size quantities. The detailers purchase most of their products in gallon containers for convenience and economy.

wheel-cleaning, and expect to wash that towel out and use it some other time for car-drying. Most detailers suggest that your drying towels be washed with bleach and detergent, but without liquid fabric softeners. Then, when you put them in your clothes dryer, use one of those anti-static softener "sheets" in with them. This may sound like a lot of attention and care to be paying to just the tools of drying off your car, but what we have outlined here comes from detailers with years of experience learning what products and methods work best. If you're serious about detailing, you'll follow their good advice.

Cleaning paint

Chances are, if this is your first serious detailing effort on your car, your paint will need some kind of cleaning. Not washing, but cleaning. We'll stress a very important point here which applies to most aspects of detailing. What we're all after is a car that really shines in all areas of paint, glass, chrome and wheels. The shine of a surface, or "reflectivity" to be more scientific, is a factor of that surface's flatness.

Your car's surfaces can look very sleek to the eye. Upon extreme closeup examination, however, they are really not flat at all but composed of minute hills and valleys. The hills and valleys reflect light at lots of various angles, which diffuses the reflectivity to varying degrees depending on how "hilly" the surface is. Here's a perfect example: if you rub a piece of sandpaper over a painted surface, the area instantly becomes dull. You have induced lots of deep hills and valleys and scattered the reflectivity. Depending on the coarseness of the sandpaper used, that surface will need a lot of work to get it back to a shine again.

You probably noticed while rinsing your car off how shiny it looks with a sheet of clear water all over it, and you may have thought to yourself "If I could only get the car to look that good all the time." You can, and that's what detailing

2.30 Today's cars are offered in brilliant colors that used to be attainable only at expensive custom-painting shops. However, all of these finishes today are basecoat/clearcoat paints that require special cleaning and protection to stay looking this great.

2.31 This is a sample of the "clearcoat-safe" products in the readily available product lines you're likely to find at your local auto supply store. You must read the product labels carefully to find out if they are safe for two-stage paints.

is all about, making the maximum of what you've got. The water in our example is acting as a surface covering which is temporarily filling in the minute scratches in your paint. The techniques and products we'll demonstrate in this book show you how to achieve that "wet look" gloss and keep it protected. The basic plan is to wash the vehicle until it is as clean as it will ever get, "surface" the paint to make it as flat as possible, then protect that gloss with clear, durable wax that will enhance that shine and guard the surface from dirt, contaminants and the other paint "disasters" we have mentioned. Once the surface is clean and flat and you keep up a good wax protection, future detailing will be only a matter of an hour or two per week. In a later part of this chapter, we will deal with flattening a really faded or damaged paint job, but for now we'll assume you have a car in typically good shape and proceed with our initial detailing.

Like sandpapers, paint cleaning products come in varying degrees of abrasiveness, from rough compounds that are used only when machine-buffing a new, wet-sanded two-stage paint job, to polishing compounds that are good for getting off stubborn spots or treating really faded paint, to fine polishes and paint "cleaners." The latter are very fine abrasives often mixed with wax and labeled "cleaner-wax" for a one-step procedure. The condition of your paint surface determines how abrasive a treatment you need to achieve the flatness we're looking for. The more abrasive the product, the more actual paint you will remove in the process of achieving flatness, and you want to remove as little paint as possible. When restoring an old, faded paint job, it can be difficult not to polish through the paint and down to the metal! Even when polishing paint with a very fine abrasive, you are still putting scratches into the surface, but they are smaller than what was there before because more of the "hills" have been taken down. In all cases, although the array of products you'll find at the store is overwhelming, you are well-served by very carefully reading the directions and cautions in the fine print on the back of the package as to the intended use of the product. The pros tell you to use the least abrasive product that seems to do the job for your application.

Most cars that have been cared for somewhat, garaged often or that are nearly new should still have plenty of paint on the surface, making the kind of paint flattening we're addressing here quite safe for the paint. There is one caveat, however. Many new cars in the past decade feature a two-stage paint, also called basecoat/clearcoat. In this process, a base color coat is applied, and then a protective coat of clear paint is applied to protect and add gloss to the base paint. They are in many cases easier to care for and maintain a shine longer than factory paint jobs of the past, but some precautions are in order.

There is some controversy among painters and detailers about the durability of the factory clearcoats. A number of vehicles of the late 1980's exhibited serious failure of their clearcoats, and on some models the car manufacturers have actually been repainting cars for free that had short-lived factory clearcoats. Some of the paint products in the stores actually warn not to use them on these paint jobs. Your factory owner's manual should tell you something about the kind of paint your car has, but it may tend to "wax" somewhat poetic and boastful about how durable it is and how little maintenance is needed. If you are unsure about whether you have a basecoat/clearcoat paint, try a little test. Use a little of the paint polishing product on a remote area like inside a door jamb **(see illustra-**

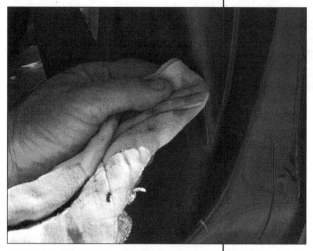

2.32 To be certain what kind of paint you have, try using polishing compound on a white cloth in the door jamb or other out-of-the-way area. If paint color shows up on your cloth, you do not have a clearcoated paint.

tion). If any paint color comes off on the polishing cloth, there's no clear protective coating. If no color comes off, then you probably have a clearcoat. Most detailers don't like to use any abrasive products on clearcoat vehicles; rather, they use products that clean chemically. The only exception would be when they have to remove overspray or some other foreign material from the surface, and they do that with extreme care and experience.

The main problem in polishing a car with a clearcoat is that you don't necessarily know when to stop since you can't see the oxidized clearcoat particles accumulating on your polishing cloth as you would with a conventional paint where your cloth right away starts to show the color of the paint you're cleaning. Since the scratches and surface imperfections we are trying to remove in obtaining a flat finish are so tiny, it wouldn't hurt at all to examine the paint close up with a strong magnifying glass in good lighting. You want to clean the surface only enough to get rid of the scratches and imperfections. Going any further may only remove more protective clearcoat.

The surface you'll see with the magnifying glass will amaze you! You'll see lots of scratches you never saw before. On conventional paint jobs (non-

2.33 Wax should be applied with a small, soft sponge or applicator pad like this. If your wax didn't come with an applicator, detailing supply sources sell them very inexpensively. When the applicator gets dirty, toss it and start with a new one.

2.34 Follow the directions on your wax container for application advice. Some products go on better with a dampened sponge. This daily-driver grocery-getter is receiving a basic coat of Meguiar's cleaner-wax, applied in the cool of the late afternoon.

2.35 Most waxes will dry to a haze and can then be buffed off with a soft cloth or home-type buffer. When using a cloth, it's very important at this stage to turn the cloth over frequently to keep exposing a clean section to the paint.

2.36 Even a basic, one hour home wash-and-wax job can deliver admirable results in terms of shine and surface protection. Once cleaned and properly waxed, the car will repel water and dirt better and be easier to clean next time. The difference between this and the "ultimate" detailing is the latter has more steps, such as polishing and glazing, and takes much longer.

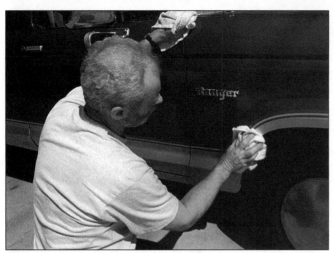

2.37 Use two cloths when buffing off your wax. One covers your other hand when you rest it on the car while rubbing the wax off with the main cloth. This prevents hand oils and acids from imprinting the surface when you unwittingly rest your hand on the just-buffed surface.

clearcoat), the pigmented (color) layer is usually deep enough to withstand the polishing-out of most scratches. Clearcoats are another story, and here's where yet another type of product comes into use: sealer and glaze. Each of these detailing products has its own uses, but the function with each type is to help fill in the minute valleys in your paint, almost like the sheets of water temporarily did when you were rinsing the just-washed vehicle.

Buffing

Note: *For more information on buffing, see Chapter 3.*

Sealers and glazes require buffing to achieve their effect, and then they must be waxed over right away or the sun and atmosphere will start immediately to dull them down. So there is considerable elbow grease involved in using them, but they are the stock-in-trade of the top professional detailers and show-car owners. There is a bewildering array of them on the market, including combination glaze/sealers, and many detailers have their personal favorites that they use exclusively. For most readers, one of the national brands in the least aggressive form would be fine, especially if you are trying to do this by hand.

As with any paint cleaner or protectant, it's best to work one small area at a time when using sealers and glazes, and they must be used in the shade on a cool painted surface. Whether working by hand or with a machine, handle an area no bigger than half the hood size of the average vehicle. The pro detailers, who must work fairly quickly and efficiently to make a living, use professional buffers whenever possible, but some of the products available can be used by hand if the directions are followed closely.

Hand buffing today, especially on sensitive clearcoats, requires that you use only the cleanest and softest, all-cotton, non-abrasive cloths. These should be given the same kind of washing and care as the cleanup towels we discussed earlier and should not be mixed with the cleanup towels. Professional cotton polishing cloths are available at automotive paint stores, and many detailers also swear by using cloth baby diapers. To really carry the polishing product well, a very open weave in the material is best. With a tight weave, sometimes the polishing material and dead paint can become "balled up" and you drag this around as you polish, putting in minute scratches instead of taking them out. The amateur's biggest mistake, other than using too aggressive a polish, is using the polishing cloth after it has become dirty and clogged with paint and dried polish. You must turn the cloth over frequently to constantly expose clean cloth to the area you are working on; don't let dried material and dirt on your cloth defeat what you are trying to do, which is to achieve clean, flat paint. If the polishing cloth doesn't come clean after washing with normal detergent in your washer, it's time to toss that cloth or relegate it to some other detailing function like wheel or engine cleaning.

To get back to using sealers and glazes, it's vitally important that you read the directions on the product before use. Of course, like any detailing product, they should be used only on cool surfaces, preferably in the shade or indoors, but with plenty of lighting so you can really see where the minute scratches are and how well you're doing on evenly glossing the surface. Mots of the glazes and combination glaze/sealer products must be buffed off before they fully dry. They often contain resins that help them fill in swirl marks left by previous polishing or compounding. Using a back-and-forth motion with your cloth to apply the product, let dry only to a semi-haze; then buff with the same motion, not a circular motion. Buff until there is a high gloss. Some of the many glazes and sealers are very tough to buff out to a gloss if you let them dry fully before buffing, so do it in the shade and make sure your phone's answering machine is on when you start the project. You'll love the results of the glaze or glaze/sealer. This may be the shiniest you've ever seen your car!

Waxing

Wax is the final line of defense in your effort to shine and protect your car's paint, and its importance can't be overstated. All of the preparation work you've invested up to this point is lost if you don't wax the vehicle thoroughly and immediately. Everything we've suggested so far is aimed at getting a clean, smooth painted surface free of scratches, tar, bug stains or any other imperfections. Now you can use a good wax to protect all that effort.

Wax products are among the most ubiquitous detailing products in national advertising, and scores of brands vie for space on the shelves at your auto supply store or retail chain.

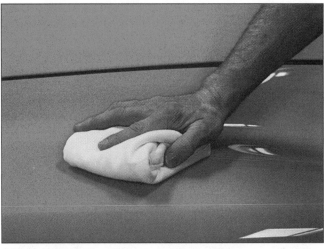

2.38 Pro detailers and showcar owners like to use soft cotton diapers to polish and wax very expensive paint jobs such as this. Keeping the cloth folded to about half-inch thickness at all times prevents the shape of your hand and fingers from causing uneven pressure on the paint when rubbing.

The key buzzword in wax has always been carnauba, a substance derived from South American plants. It is a natural wax that is very hard and can withstand high temperatures, like on the hood of your car on a hot day. Carnauba in pure form is fairly expensive, and you'll find that generally the more expensive waxes have more carnauba in them. The substance has enough mystique about it that it is *the* marketing ingredient for car-care products, and you'll find the word carnauba used on products that contain very little natural carnauba wax. Always check the label for specific contents.

Those products that have high levels of carnauba will most likely give you the best shine and the longest protection, up to as long as 3-6 months. Their labels will most likely state that these waxes are intended only for use on cleaned, polished paint. It would be a waste of time to apply good carnauba over a dirty or dull paint.

2.39 Only the right side of this paint section had been properly treated with quality carnauba wax, which is why the paint is beading up there, indicating that the paint is well-protected. The true carnauba paste waxes are admittedly a little more work to apply but offer the longest-lasting protection.

If you have followed through with us so far on washing and polishing your paint, then we recommend that you not "wimp out" on elbow grease at this final stage of waxing. Use a carnauba paste wax. The carnauba has to be thinned considerably to be put into spray-waxes and liquid waxes. Obviously, the liquids and sprays are faster and easier to apply, but generally offer less protection and may not have the deep gloss of buffed carnauba wax. Apply the wax of your choice following the manufacturer's directions, usually with a back-and-forth motion with a slightly-dampened cotton terry cloth. Many detailers also use cloth baby diapers cut into small sections for applying wax, and some use cheesecloth because it carries so much product when applying wax. Some waxes comes with a foam applicator in the can, or you can buy separate small sponges or foam pads specifically designed for applying wax. These other products are only for applying wax, not buffing it - cloth is still the proper material for hand buffing.

Most wax manufacturers recommend two light coats rather than one thick application. A thick coat of wax is very difficult to buff off properly, especially if it's carnauba. If you have already done the glaze/sealer process, you have filled in the minute scratches in the finish, and probably only need one coat of wax to protect it all. The sealers, glazes and waxes all contain resins and oils to "feed" the paint and keep it from drying out and oxidizing. Think of detailing as "skin care" for your car.

When waxing around areas such as chrome trim, fender emblems, antenna, etc., you should be cautious not to build up too much wax in the joints of mating surfaces. It may attract dirt later on and also can be hard to remove from detailed areas of trim without tedious work.

The end result is going to be a finish that you'll find well worth all the efforts you've expended. During all of the foregoing detailing procedures, there is considerable hand labor involved. You have to block out plenty of time to complete these steps, and the products you use and the effort you put in is going to depend on just how sharp you want the vehicle to look. Some busy people prefer to do the whole procedure only on one section of the car at a time, like the top surfaces one weekend, and the sides and front and rear the next weekend. Use whatever schedule works for you, but remember that an area that is washed, cleaned and glazed needs to be waxed right away. If you wait until the next weekend for the waxing, the environment will have already affected the finish and you may have to start over again to be ready for waxing.

Only you can determine how much time is worth the effort. What we have described above is a procedure for really premium gloss and protection. You may be too busy for that, or maybe you're not keeping the car very long. There are much easier products to use when you want a simple wash'n'wax - you would skip the cleaning, polishing or glazing of the paint, and their attendant buffing, and just use a cleaner/wax after washing. This will offer some protection of the paint and a reasonable shine. Easiest of all detailing products to use are the liquid cleaner/waxes, which are both easy to apply and easy to buff off. The result will look good, but the shine will not be as deep. Most of the scratches and imperfections will still be there, and the wax protection won't last long.

It's easy to tell how much wax protection you have when you are washing your vehicle. How the rinse water looks on the surface of the car tells you a lot about the presence of waxes and resins protecting the paint. If the water beads up all over the finish, then it is still protected against the elements **(see illustration)**. If however, the water runs off easily in flat sheets, you don't have enough protection and it's time to re-wax the vehicle. How long the protection lasts depends on the weather and the amount and type of detailing, particularly the final waxing.

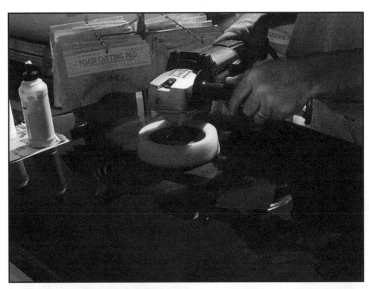

3

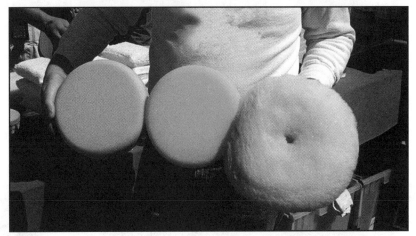

Buffing

3 Buffing

There are only a few situations in which a buffer is required in detailing. The first is when a brand new custom paint job has been applied (acrylic enamel with hardener) and it has been color-sanded to remove tiny imperfections and level "orange peel" in the paint. Color-sanding refers to wet-sanding the entire paint job with ultra-fine #600 and then #1200 sandpaper to achieve a flat finish. This surface is capable of showing a fantastic shine but only after buffing with rubbing compound, then a glazing and a waxing.

3.1 When a professional detail shop has to turn ugly duckling used cars into creampuffs on a daily basis, a powerful electric buffer is a must to get the workload out. Note here that the operator has applied the liquid glazing compound directly onto the paint and is now buffing it in. Some detailers prefer to apply the polishes and waxes directly to the buffer pad, then buff into the paint.

The second reason could be that industrial smog or overspray has attacked the paint and the only solution is to buff the paint back to life. The usual reason that buffing is done in a detail shop is to restore really neglected paint. If your paint is in good shape now, we don't recommend you use a buffer at all, especially on sensitive clearcoats. There is nothing an electric buffer can do that can't be done by hand with the right polishing products; it will just take longer and require considerable elbow grease to get the job done. But there is no doubt that the buffer can speed up the whole process.

Unfortunately, electric buffers can also be dangerous, especially in novice hands. A professional, variable-speed (from 1500-3000 rpm) buffer is quite expensive and should be used carefully by someone with experience; otherwise, the finish can be buffed through when the machine hits a fender ridge or other body detail. As fast as a buffer goes,

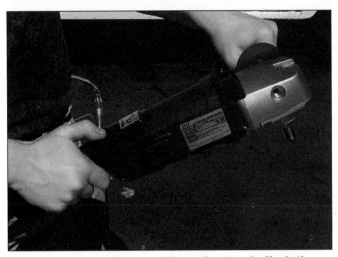

3.2 This Black & Decker right-angle rotary buffer is the standard tool in pro detailing shops. It's rugged, relatively compact, and features a variable-speed switch right in the top of the handle. The operator can adjust the speed anytime while buffing.

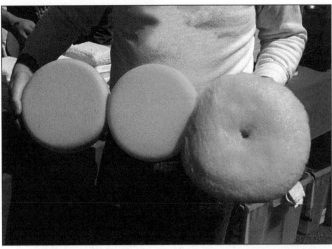

3.3 At right here is a standard sheepskin buffing pad, while to its left are the newer foam buffing pads. Varying densities of the foam give these pads different characteristics: a hard one for compounding, softer ones for fine polish and waxes.

especially when an aggressive compound is being used, it is very easy to cut right through clearcoat, basecoat, primer and right down to bare metal. Pro detailers use variable-speed buffers that feature the speed control right on the handle, so they can vary the speed while buffing, slowing down when they get to sensitive areas. With a heavy-duty buffer in the hands of an experienced professional, it is amazing to watch the metamorphosis of an aging car becoming new-looking again, panel by panel, with the heavy, humming machine seeming to glide over the surface while the operator constantly adjusts the speed up and down depending on the curves and ridges he comes across. The pro-type buffing machine isn't going to be worth the expense for the average person, unless he plans to make a little extra weekend money by detailing other people's cars, and he should have some solid experience before he machine-buffs his neighbor's new car!

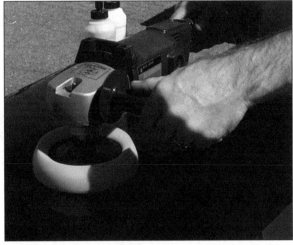

3.4 In this effective demonstration, a detailer is buffing on a "junkyard" hood with a foam pad and compound. Before the buffing, he had purposely dry-sanded the area with sandpaper to dull and scratch the paint.

Anything that the machine can do, your hands can do; it's just going to require more effort and time to get the same results, and close attention must be paid to consistency of your efforts - not rubbing too much here and not enough there. There are "consumer-type" buffers for sale in most auto stores and retail department stores that work fairly well and generally operate slowly enough to not be dangerous to your paint when used judiciously and with the right level of abrasiveness in the product you're buffing. Those that oscillate rather than just rotate (called orbital buffers or waxers) usually leave less swirl marks and scratches. Such buffers are more commonly used to apply glazes and waxes rather than aggressive compounds. They are used by many consumers to both apply and buff out final waxes, although some experts claim that hand-buffing of the final wax coat is always better done by hand. As it is, there will be many areas on the car where the polishing, glazing, waxing or buffing must all be done by hand anyway due to the shape prohibiting the use of a buffer.

Buffing paint has come a long way from the early days of the automobile. Remember the old saying attributed to Henry Ford I in talking about his Model T? He said the customer could have his Ford "in any color he wants, so long as it's

black." In the early days, it wasn't just an economy move on Ford's part. The earliest car and carriage paints were mixtures of shellac and lampblack. Even on Ford's primitive first assembly line, this was applied by hand with brushes and then rubbed out by hand later with a mixture of fine pumice stone in water, like an early-day rubbing compound. Later when spray equipment and better paints came along, Mr. Ford, who was known as a mechanical genius rather than a fashion kind of guy, still insisted his cars be all black, only relenting during the Depression when competition forced him to offer other colors.

Machine buffing has always been done with genuine or imitation wool bonnets over the head of the buffer. Until recent years, this was the only choice of pad material for applying all types of paint detailing products. The "bite" of such bonnets from the nap of the material could often put as many fine scratches into a paint job as it took out, and there has always been a good market for "swirl-remover" glazes to follow polishing with a buffer. The other drawback when using wool pads was that, in getting too close to a piece of chrome trim or a light bezel, the nap of the wool material could get caught on a sharp projection and the torque of the buffer would almost toss the operator across the room.

Many painters and detailers still use wool pads, especially when buffing out a color-sanded, new paint job, but an alternative has come along in the form of foam buffer pads. The foam pads are relatively inexpensive, feature quick-attaching Velcro backing for easy changes on the buffer and, best of all, their hardness is adjustable. There are varying grades of foam pads sold today. A relatively hard foam pad might be used for really aggressive work in compounding faded paint, to be followed by a softer foam pad that is used to apply glazes and sealers, and an even softer pad that is useful for fine polish and waxes. They are said to be much more controllable than the old pads, and the worst that can happen when you get close to a sharp piece of trim is that all of a sudden there are particles of foam flying around. Aside from the outer edge, the rest of the pad is still useable. There have been few advances in buffing technology in 40 years, but the foam pads are definitely a step forward.

3.5 After a minute with the foam pad and compound, the center of the "ruined" area already looks great. You can see the unbuffed areas on either side.

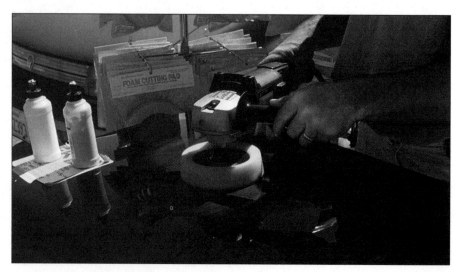

3.6 The demonstration is complete when the detailer switches to a softer foam pad and fine polish, which together restore the section of paint to better-looking than before he scratched up the hood.

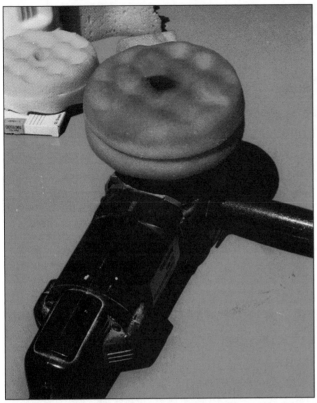

3.7 Some of the foam pads now available have two sides, with different densities of foam. This one has a side with a "waffle" pattern, which is said to reduce the heat buildup on the paint surface while buffing.

3.8 Here among the wash wands and car vacuums in this store's display are the orbital-type buffers recommended for amateur home use, for both minor polishing and for applying and buffing off waxes.

3.9 Wax manufacturers such as Eagle One recommend using an orbital buffer like this because it leaves less swirl marks and turns 1800 or less rpms. Their advice is to use the orbital for applying and working in glazes and waxes. Wax removal should still be done by hand.

3.10 A trick from Eagle One is to apply some of their Ultra Glaze and carnauba paste wax at the same time, by working the glaze into the buffer cloth first and then spreading the wax on like buttering a piece of toast. After it hazes on the car, use soft cotton towels to buff.

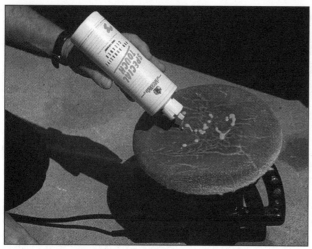

3.11 Here a glaze is being applied to the "applicator" pad of an orbital polisher. The applicator pad has a sealed backing for use with liquid-type products.

3.12 When using aggressive products, even with an orbital polisher, swirl marks can still show up if you use too much pressure on the surface. The orbital's manufacturer recommends letting the weight of the machine provide all the pressure against the paint. Even so, the orbital marks are easily removed with machine or hand-buffed glaze and final wax.

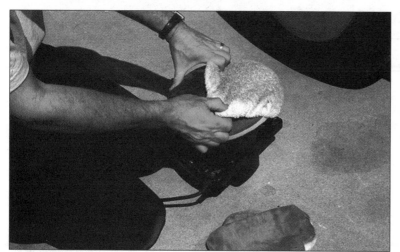

3.13 Terrycloth pad covers come with most orbital machines. The ones with sealed backings are for applying products; the softer, unbacked ones are for buffing off dried products. The covers are washable.

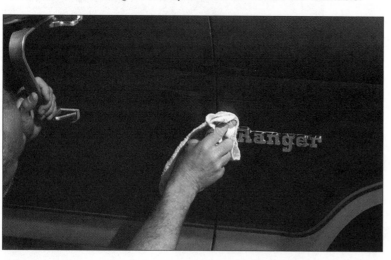

3.14 Even a vehicle that is already shiny can benefit from an orbital buffer, which can be used to both apply and remove your final wax coats.

3.15 No matter what type of buffer you use, the final work has to be done by hand, both for places where the buffer can't reach and where there are ridges and other vulnerable spots you don't want to buff through.

4

Using the coin-op carwash

4 Using the coin-op carwash

Washing the family car on a Saturday morning has been as American a tradition as fireworks on the 4th of July. Some choose to go to the regular carwash and listen to the oldies on the speaker system, watching through the glass as their car goes down a "cleanliness assembly line" to finally emerge clean into the sunshine where attendants wipe it down. Others make a regular ritual of doing the whole process in their driveway, and on Saturday and Sunday mornings during good weather there is hardly a dry gutter to be found in suburban America. Sometime since the 1950s, an alternative that seems to offer the best of both traditions has been appealing to yet a third group, those who choose the do-it-yourself, coin-operated car wash.

The fact that you have to pay for each fraction of a minute of wash time by inserting quarters into a machine makes the coin-op carwash the least leisurely of the three carwash options, but the resultant speed and efficiency may be the main factors which attract customers there. Besides being quicker than a home wash or pro carwash, the coin-op offers high-pressure spray with a "wand" that can dispense a variety of waters, soap and even liquid wax. Although the pressure is higher (900 psi), the volume of water (3-6 gallons per minute) used is less than that used in a carwash at home, where as many as 10 gallons per minute may flood the driveway. The coinwash carries with it a sort of patriotic edge during times of drought and water conservation. The coin-op carwash also has the do-it-yourself feature to it that appeals to many who still want to take an active hand in their car cleanliness. If there's a little extra mud under the fenderwells this week, you can put a few extra quarters in and concentrate on that area. You may even decide to bring a can of Gunk down with you and clean off the engine compartment while you're there. It's the next-best thing to a steam-cleaning for getting grime off of engines and chassis, although some coin-op carwashes prohibit engine washing in their bays.

We spoke to the owner of a coin-operated carwash to find out the right and wrong way to take advantage of the system. He said "a lot of people waste their money here, using many more quarters than they need to." They can save themselves some problems first of all by just carefully reading the posted signs at the coin-op. The scrubbing phase is where most people waste their quarters, thinking that the machine has to be on the whole time they are scrubbing the car.

Depositing a pile of quarters earns you (in the case of our subject carwash) about four minutes and five seconds, so the time must be spent wisely. Once you have done this a few times, you'll have a better feel for how long each phase of the washing should take. Most coin stalls have a machine with a dial from which to choose: rinse, soap, wax or final rinse. If you follow our photo sequence, you'll see the best procedure to get the most out of your coin-op wash.

Using the coin-op carwash

4.1 A modern coin-operated carwash installation which has six drivethrough bays so there is little waiting period on busy days, plus two extra-tall bays on the right for trucks and RVs.

4.2 The most important piece of equipment at the coin-op carwash is the bill changer that takes paper money and gives back quarters because everything here is coin-operated, including the wash equipment, the vacuum and the dispensers that vend small artificial chamois. Note also the wringer for removing excess water from your chamois after leaving the wash bay.

4.3 This basically dirty but not abused Toyota was a perfect subject for our use of the coin-op carwash.

4.4 The process begins with your car in the center of the bay and you inserting the required amount of quarters and selecting "Rinse" on the selector.

4.5 Very quickly you get the whole car wet with water, switching to "Soap" about 15 seconds before you're done with the wetting process, since there is a 15-second delay when switching over before the next product comes out the pressure wand.

4.6 Switch the dial now to "Brush" and use the soap-dispersing brush to soap up the car, starting from the top down.

4.7 Get as much of the soapsuds on the vehicle as possible, even if you run out of time on the machine. Try for even distribution of the suds on the car's exterior.

4.8 Once the car has been covered with suds, don't put any more quarters in the machine. Just take your time to use the soapy brush to scrub all areas of the vehicle. You are loosening all the dirt and road film on the car and keeping it in suspension with the thick suds. Bays in most coin-op carwashes are fully shaded, so the sun isn't as much of a factor in drying out the soapsuds.

4.9 Take the time to scrub the rocker panels, below both bumpers and the wheels/tires, especially if you have accumulated any mud.

4.10 Now insert some more quarters and switch the control to "Rinse." Good carwashes are using softened water in all their water cycles which reduces the spotting problem greatly.

4.11 The pressure wand still emits at high pressure on the Rinse cycle, making quick work of hosing off all the soap and loosened dirt. Again rinse from the top down.

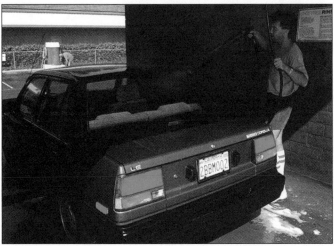

4.12 Quickly switch to "Wax" which will deposit liquid wax on the car along with plenty of softened water. Then allow the car to stand for a moment.

4.13 Now switch to "Final Rinse" which employs an even further treated water that doesn't leave harsh spots and comes out a lower pressure than any of the other selections on the dial. Aim it to "sheet" water across flat areas, and it won't take much water to rinse off the whole car.

4.14 You can dry the car right there, while parked next to the vacuuming machines, or dry the car off by driving it around the block, which gets rid of 80% of the excess water, then using towels for the rest before using the coin-op vacuums to clean the carpets and upholstery.

Notes

5

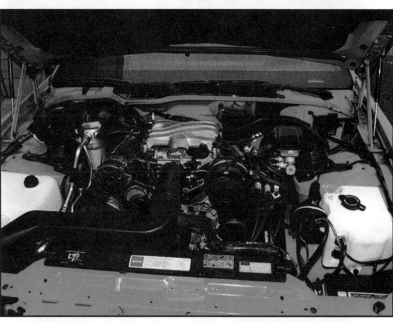

The three-hour pro detail

5 The three-hour pro detail

A professional detailing shop is usually a very busy place. The bulk of the work in such a shop is performed for area car dealerships, with the remainder of business for private party cars. Since dealers bring in so much business, the detail shops like to offer them good service and good turnaround time, which the dealers appreciate because speed means a quicker turnaround of their inventory. They buy cars wholesale at auctions or acquire them from their own new-car dealership trade-ins, and they normally need to get the cars thoroughly reconditioned so they can be immediately put out for sale on the used-car lot. They make considerable profit on such cars, and this is in no small part due to the quality of the detailing service they use. Their trade-ins usually come in looking well-used and go back on the lot after the detailing process looking like they had been kept in a hermetically-sealed garage since new.

The photo sequence shown here was shot at a typical detailing shop where they have both a permanent "base" shop and several mobile detailing units out in the field. Expensive specialty cars and cars detailed for dealerships are generally done in the shop, while private party "basic wash and wax" jobs are handled by the mobile units.

The subject car was a red Pontiac Firebird that the dealer wanted back the same day. It was a Friday, and he knew that, with beautiful weather forecast for the weekend, he would have no trouble selling a sporty red car with aluminum wheels and a V6, if it looked decent. It didn't. The red paint, a color very subject to fading from ultraviolet light exposure, was quite dull, the interior had an odor to it, the carpeting was dirty, the windows were a mess and the engine showed every one of its miles.

What follows is what a typical detailing shop did in three hours. Some of the cleaning was done by one person, and part of the time two were working together on the interior cleaning and paint restoration. The difference was remarkable. You couldn't help but be tempted to buy the car after seeing it finished, so thoroughly had the "makeover" been performed. We illustrate the process here to show you what can be expected in a thorough detailing at a professional shop. A private party could have paid for many extra services that are not shown here, but this is the basic treatment for dealership vehicles.

The three-hour pro detail

5.1 Everyone likes to pop the hood open when shopping for a used car, so the first step in detailing a car for dealership sale is to steam-clean the engine and engine compartment. Before the hot water spraying begins, the dirtiest spots have been pre-soaked with a degreaser spray. Note the detailer is wearing sunglasses. This isn't just for style; he's protecting his eyes from splashback of hot water and chemicals.

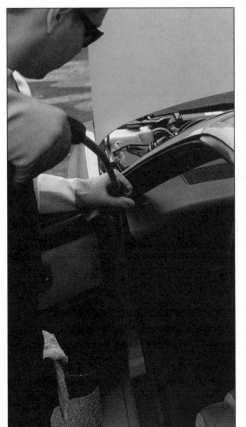

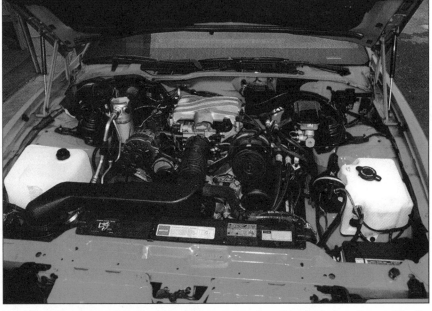

5.2 After the steam-cleaning, the engine compartment looked almost new. Plastic parts, cast aluminum and painted components all looked fresh. The pro detailers try not to use harsh chemical cleaners that can dull paint and components.

5.3 While he has the steam-clean machine running, Jeremy is blasting steam into other areas, such as the wheels, tires, wheelwells, front suspension, and here into the front edge of the door jamb behind the front fenders.

5.4 Jeremy sprays everything underhood with dressing. In this case, it is not the usual alcohol-based protectants that we amateurs use for tires and bumpers but a thin, water-based dressing that imparts a shine to almost anything it touches. For home use, regular protectants applied just to the appropriate components will provide longer-lasting looks and protection.

5.5 A spritz of dressing under the hood itself dresses up an area dulled by engine heat, as well as making the factory decals look new again.

5.6 When everything is dry underhood, about 20 minutes later, the transformation is complete, and without reading the odometer, you would have no idea how old this engine and compartment are.

5.7 After the steam cleaning has removed the grime from the fenderwells, John spritzs some dressing into the fenderwells, which makes the black factory undercoating look like it had been applied only last week. It's little details like this that add up to a total look of rejuvenation for the car.

5.8 In this case, the Firebird's aluminum wheels were clear-coated, so they didn't require polishing. The steam-cleaner removed all the road grime and disc brake dust, and John squirts both tires and wheels with dressing.

5.9 Turning now to the interior, Jeremy blows out all nooks, crannies and crevices with an airhose and blower nozzle. In many cases, this is faster and easier than trying to get every speck of dust with rags and protectant and certainly takes care of all loose dirt.

5.10 Jeremy uses a short bristle brush and lacquer thinner to remove black scuff marks from the door sill area and the kick panels. The brush and thinner soften the marks which are then wiped off with a rag. Stubborn spots require a follow-up with vinyl cleaner.

5.11 Carpet cleaning is very important in detailing a car for sale, and in this case the car also had an "off" odor that needed eliminating. Instead of thin carpet-cleaning sprays, the detailer uses a bucket of soapy shampoo, which is applied unsparingly with a wash mitt in one hand while the other hand follows close behind with a stiff brush to work the suds in and loosen dirt.

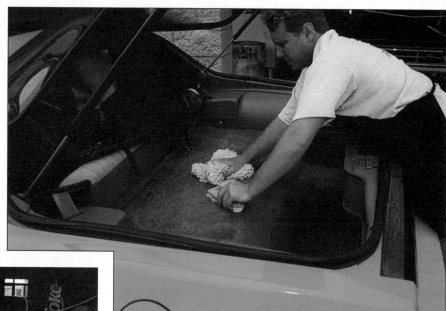

5.12 Even before the carpeting and upholstery are completely dry, vacuuming of the complete interior begins with an industrial wet/dry vacuum, which helps speed up the detailing process by helping to dry the interior more quickly.

5.13 John takes extra time to use the vacuum's crevice tool and get any dirt around the seat tracks, carpet edges, door sills and any hard-to-get-at spot where dirt could have been overlooked for some time.

5.14 Vinyl protectant is sprayed on all interior panels and wiped down with a cloth in the other hand. What's important here is getting rid of all dust and having a uniform sheen on the surfaces.

5.15 John and Jeremy work as a team to apply and buff polish and glaze onto the Firebird's faded paint. John applies the product, staying just ahead of the buffing machine which is fitted with a light foam pad. It's the efficiency of this kind of teamwork that allows the pros to do in three hours what it would take the rest of us all day to perform.

5.16 The final paint treatment is a quality wax applied by hand and allowed to haze all over the car. At this point the wax can be applied very quickly, because, since the windows and trim haven't been cleaned, overlapping of the wax isn't important.

5.17 The wax treatment is buffed off by hand with clean terry cloths. In the background are private party cars being readied for carshow entry with paint "pampering" and airbrush touchups.

5.18 Finally, both men go over the entire car with clean cloths, checking for any imperfections in the paint or trim. They also go over all seams with detailing brushes to remove wax residue.

5.19 The last step is to bring the car outside into the sun for final cleaning of the windows and a last look around the car. Preliminary glass cleaning can be done indoors, but it takes strong sunlight to see all the smudges on both sides of the glass, so the final glass cleaning is always done outdoors. Note how John is cleaning the upper edge of the glass, while using another cloth to keep his left hand from making any new smudges.

Exterior
details

6 Exterior details

Our basic wash-polish-wax procedure in Chapter 2 covered taking care of 75% of your exterior detailing, the paint itself. However, there is a myriad of other areas to be addressed, too. With the paint cleaned and protected, your attention can then be turned, as your own schedule permits, to details such as the bumpers, chrome trim, grille area, lights, window glass, exterior rubber parts and even weather-stripping. An additional consideration if your vehicle is a convertible would be the care and cleaning of the convertible top, including its plastic rear window, or care of padded vinyl tops on hardtop cars.

Bumpers and chrome

It used to be that "bumpers" and "chrome" would be synonymous in terms of detailing procedures, but cars in the last ten years show less and less chrome and more of other materials such as plastic, rubber and even plastic-coated steel. Some cars have a basically chromed-steel bumper with a vinyl or rubber "rub-strip" insert and a plastic panel between the bumper and body, while other models exhibit just the opposite treatment, they have a no-chrome basic treatment with perhaps a small chrome trim strip added through the center.

Regardless of the materials or style of bumpers you have, you must use the detailing materials and techniques that are matched to the surface material you are working on. Most chrome cleaners, for instance, are designed for chromed

6.1 There are many aspects to detailing the exterior of a vehicle besides the basic paint. Unless the trim, top, bumpers and glass receive the same level of attention, the overall impression will still be that the owner or detailer just didn't go 100%.

metal and don't work best for the chromed plastic trim many cars feature today. Always read the instructions on the back of the product before you buy to make sure it's compatible with the surface you're working on. While a detailing "kit" could have at one time contained just chrome polish and paint polish/wax, there are now many kinds of products needed to keep pace with upkeep of the variety of surfaces now on cars.

The main purpose of detailing we have already described for the paint applies equally to bumpers and trim - get the surface as clean as possible, then protect it with wax or other protectants. As with paint, when you get a good "baseline" the car will be much easier to maintain in the future. For standard chrome-plated metal bumpers and other similar trim, there is a variety of chrome cleaners on the market. Check the instructions for how abrasive the product is. Many of the products we'll describe later for wheel care can be successfully used on chrome trim to get down to a really clean, shiny surface.

The cautions we gave you about the thin nature of today's two-stage paints apply to chrome metal surfaces as well. Traditional chrome-plating of metal parts is a three-stage process. First the part is plated with copper and the copper layer is then polished. The copper acts like primer/surfacer does when painting, providing a polishable layer that smoothes out minor imperfections and fills minute scratches in the surface. After the copper, the part is then nickel-plated, which is the equivalent of the "body color" step in painting, and when buffed the nickel gives the part the beautiful reflective shine we associate with chrome. Unfortunately, the buffed nickel finish is very susceptible to the elements and will tarnish rather quickly without protection. The final step is a thin plating of chrome, which protects the nickel much like a clear-coat does over the body-color in painting. That topmost layer of chrome is quite thin, and you can polish through it if you aren't careful. You may have seen gray or light brown spots or discolorations on bumpers of older cars, say from the Sixties. These are spots where, either from neglect or too much polishing, the chrome layer is no longer protecting the nickel.

The standard caution is to use only the level of aggressiveness in cleaning that it takes to do the job, no more. Start with the least-aggressive (least abrasive content) product, and, if that doesn't get it clean, only then go on to heavier cleaners. As with paint, there are chrome cleaners specifically for deep cleaning of really neglected chrome. These should be used only in tough cases, and you have to be careful not to rub through that protective layer. In some cases of rusted or pitted chrome, you can't help but use the aggressive product to get the rust or discoloration off, but that part will need immediate protection with several coats of carnauba wax to keep corrosion from coming back right away. Only by keeping a constant watch on those areas, and cleaning and waxing as necessary, can you forestall the inevitable rechroming of the part.

Plastic chrome trim is increasingly in evidence on vehicles as manufacturers try to get cars lighter and cheaper **(see illustration)**. The trim looks great when new, but the surface electroplating is even thinner than real chrome on steel. To clean it, use only non-abrasive products that specifically state they are for use on nonmetallic chrome parts. Once clean, protect such trim with good wax and it should last for many years. If yours does become damaged, scratched or faded, it can be replaced if the vehicle is new enough for the dealer to still list the part in his catalog, or you can have it rechromed.

Rechroming of plastic parts was once thought of as pos-

6.2 Although it looks like real steel, many car and truck emblems today are just chrome-plated plastic and should not be treated with regular metal chrome polish.

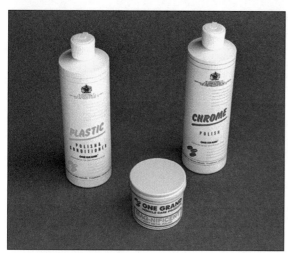

6.3 There are lots of chrome cleaners available. These are from One Grand and include a plastic polish (good for lenses and plastic chrome), a regular chrome polish, and a mag wheel polish useful for stainless trim, non-anodized aluminum and neglected chrome.

6.4 Only the left (in photo) side of this truck's bumper and spoiler have been cleaned. Both chromed steel and black vinyl needed detailing.

6.6 Basic car-washing soap should be worked in with a plastic (fingernail) brush as a first step. Do this to both the chrome and the grain of the vinyl areas.

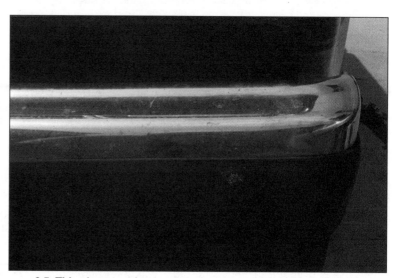

6.5 This close-up shows what chrome looks like that has been neglected. It isn't rusty yet or worn through the upper chrome coating, but it isn't very shiny, either.

6.7 After the wash, the chrome and rubber look better, but not perfect. The grime and bug smears are gone, but both materials don't show full "life."

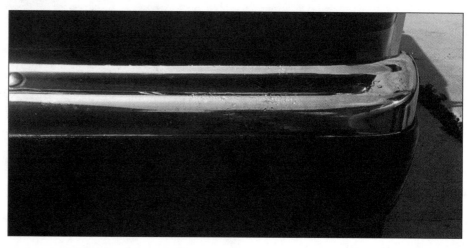

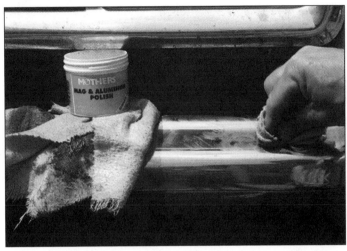

6.8 Normally, a metal polish isn't used on chrome (this is Mothers Mag Polish), but this case required removing some corroded spots where rust could begin and got the entire bumper to a "base" state of clean.

6.9 A good grade of carnauba paste wax was used to follow the cleaning, offering long-lasting protection and easy cleanups in the future.

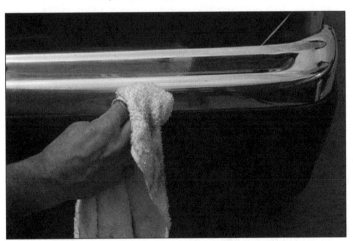

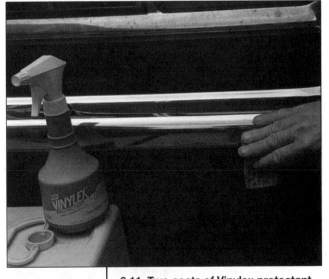

6.10 Looking at the right side of the photo where the wax has been buffed off, you can see that the bumper will now look as clean and reflective as it was intended.

6.11 Two coats of Vinylex protectant were applied with a small piece of sponge, which allows for a clean application of the dressing right up close to the chrome part without getting on the steel. You should use a variety of different-colored sponges when performing your detailing. Then you will always know that you have used the blue sponge for waxing, the yellow for protectant, etc.

6.12 A final cloth wipe of the vinyl on the bumper and the lower front spoiler to even out the second coat of protectant and the bumper is done. Bug splatters and dirt will not stick as easily in the future.

6.13 Short-bristled detailer's brushes are excellent for cleaning wax residue from along creases and around trim, like this marker lens or V-6 emblem. You can shorten the fibers on a regular paintbrush to achieve the same effect, or wrap duct tape around a brush to make the effective bristle length about this long.

sible only at the big-manufacturer end of the business, but several independent sources have sprung up in the last five years (see the Sourcelist) to service the growing trend of restoring collectible Sixties and Seventies cars. Have your part rechromed only if a new part isn't available anymore. Chromed plastic is often used today on grilles, and, when yours is at the point where it needs rechroming, chances are the structure itself isn't what it once was, with cracks, scratches and other damage. Buying a new grille will be perfect and saves having to re-paint accent areas on your old one if you have it rechromed.

When waxing your chrome parts and trim, try not to apply too much wax around emblems and edges where trim meets the body. An accu-mulation of wax in these areas is an invitation for dirt to gather and for eventual corrosion, not to mention the unsightliness of white, dried-wax residue in all those crevices. Pro detailers preparing a car for a show go to great pains with Q-tips and toothbrushes to clean wax buildup from around emblems and trim **(see illustrations)**. When you've done that tedious work a few times, you learn not to apply so much wax near the trim in the first place!

Another type of exterior metal trim your vehicle may have is aluminum or stainless steel. There isn't as much of the latter on cars as there once was, but it is extremely resistant to the elements and easy to clean with standard metal pol-ishes. It's almost a goofproof trim material because, unless you dent it, it stays looking great forever with good care. Stainless trim has no fragile surface coat-ing, so even scratches can be polished out without danger of cutting through to a base metal beneath. Most older cars had stainless trim.

Aluminum is another story. It has been popular for years as trim material but is rapidly being replaced on most cars (high-end cars being the exceptions) with lighter and cheaper plastics. Your aluminum trim could be treated (anodized or plastic-coated) or untreated. Uncoated aluminum can deteriorate and even pit badly if neglected long enough, but in most cases it merely dulls slightly and can be restored to new brightness with metal polish, then protected with wax. Anodized and plastic-coated aluminum must be handled with care. Use only "plastic polish" with no abrasives or you can cut through the surface coating.

Black anodized aluminum trim is found often on imported sports cars. It has a rich, performance look to it when new and, kept clean and protected, can last for years. When neglected, the black fades to a dull gray and even cleaners can't bring it back. Your only choice then is to either remove it and have it stripped and reanodized at a specialty plating shop (hard to find), or you can simply repaint it black. The newer semi-gloss or "semi-flat" black spray paints look great on trim and are often used for a different look on trim that was previously bright metal color. Just clean the part thoroughly with a wax-and-grease remover, mask off the surfaces around the

6.14 Many late-model vehicles feature non-glare, blackened-out windshield wiper arms. Eventually sand and other airborne particles "sandblast" the surface, but they can be made to look like new again with a spray can of semi-flat black paint.

trim part and spray. Two or three light coats are always better than one heavy coat. It's an easy way to give a new, non-glare "sporty" look to your old windshield wiper arms, too **(see illustration)**.

Care must be used in cleaning any trim, regardless of material or product. When the trim piece is a plastic emblem or aluminum window trim, and you are doing some serious cleaning, you may want to mask off the surrounding painted areas to avoid getting cleaning products on your paint. They will probably strip your wax protection off at the very least and, if allowed to accumulate for any length of time on your paint, could cause streaking or discoloration. It's best to apply the cleaner or protectant you are using by putting it on a cloth or pad and then applying, rather than spraying it on the surface first and getting overspray on unwanted areas.

Rubber and plastic

The rubber trim used on and around your bumpers varies in hardness, and sometimes seems to defy your best efforts to either clean or protect. The smoother, vinyl-like trim is easily detailed with a number of popular interior and exterior vinyl cleaners and protectants. There are some plastic-bodied applicators with a spongelike tip that make applying protectant a cleaner job by dispensing just a little material at a time just where you want it **(see illustration).** Some of the black rubber trim on bumpers is more dense than other rubber (like tires), and protectant hardly seems to penetrate its surface. The pro advice is to treat such hard rubber with protectant and let it stay on for at least an hour before buffing. It may take several applications to get enough protectant "soaked in" for a satisfactory finish. Once treated, that area should be easier to maintain in the future. Also look for special products that are made to renew the depth of color in black rubber parts specifically - they can really bring these parts back to life. When applying protectant to rubber trim that is immediately next to chrome, glass or paint, use a Q-tip with a little protectant on it **(see illustration)**. The swab is excellent

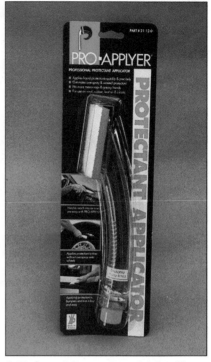

6.15 One of the most useful detailing tools we've seen is this protectant applicator from One Grand Products. Detailing exterior or interior rubber and vinyl is done faster with this tool and with less overspray.

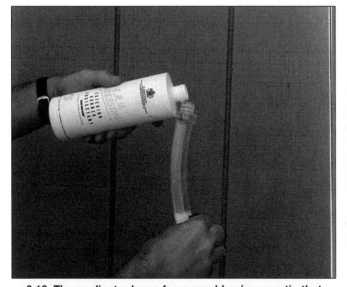

6.16 The applicator has a foam scrubber/sponge tip that applies protectant or glass cleaner as you move it when in contact with part of the vehicle. The handle can be filled with vinyl protectant, glass cleaner or leather dressing. It is very handy in dressing tires without getting protectant on the wheels.

6.17 Household cotton swabs should be in anyone's "detail bag." They are perfect for cleaning in tight areas or applying small amounts of protectant to rubber trim that is next to paint or chrome.

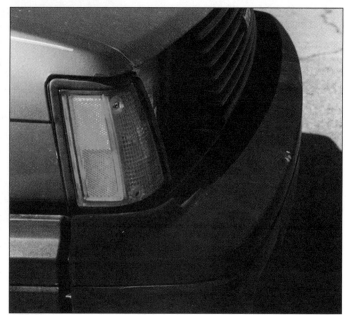

6.19 Cars that have all-rubber bumpers and are exposed to UV radiation 24 hours a day (not garaged) will eventually show weathering like this on the exposed rubber.

6.18 Wiper blades should be washed simply with carwash soap and a sponge, or an SOS pad if it has some dead rubber along the edge. Do not use any protectant or other product on the blades; it makes them glide over water rather than remove it.

for putting protectant just where you want it, and when the cotton gets dirty turn it around or toss it.

Some rubber parts that should not receive protectant are your windshield wiper blades (or headlight or rear window wipers). Simply scrub them with a toothbrush when washing the car **(see illustration)**. As long as they are kept clean of imbedded dirt, that's as much as you can do, protectants seem to interfere with the wipers' ability to clear the windshield. The wipers just glide too easily.

All exterior rubber needs basic cleaning, then regular applications of protectant to maintain its color, softness and resistance to stains, smog, etc. Nothing makes that like-new impression after detailing like the contrast between your glossy paint and the accompanying trim and rubber when the latter are cared for as much as the paint. Pro detailers often get into some very minor details when doing their work, such as cleaning and protecting the little rubber gaskets between the exterior door handles and the body, or the black rubber gasket under the car's antenna. That's why they call it detailing - the sum of all those little touches adds up to make quite an impression. Observers can see a vehicle with a nicely-waxed paint job, but, when they see the details overlooked, the impression left is still one that the car's owner just didn't go 100%.

There are a lot of applications for plastic polish on your vehicle you may not have thought of, including taillight and turn signal lenses and outside mirrors that are either painted plastic or black plastic. You don't normally think of doing anything more to a taillight lens than just washing it, but this plastic is exposed to not only the environment but elevated temperatures from the warm bulbs. The plastic can dull with weathering but is easily brought

6.20 When a bumper is this deteriorated (not just faded but covered with "dead" rubber), the best approach is to scrub briskly with a stiff brush and soap and water, let dry and then apply exterior rubber protectant.

6.21 Two coats of One Grand's ERV (exterior rubber and vinyl) were required to restore this Toyota rear bumper, with the first coat allowed to soak into the surface (in the shade) for an hour. The second coat was mainly to even out the new smooth-and-semi-glossy appearance. Coating really faded bumpers in the sun will result in streaks and non-uniform gloss.

6.22 Bumper stickers and decals can be difficult to remove, sometimes requiring careful scraping with a razor to remove the adhesive. A safer first step is to soften the old adhesive with rubber-cement thinner (available at art supply stores). A second coat of thinner usually removes the adhesive without any damage to chrome or glass (don't try it on paint!).

back with plastic polish, which helps clean the surface and correct minute scratches, and the occasional application of protectant to put back the gloss and depth of color. Further detailing of taillight lenses could be repainting any accent lines on the lens, using a small brush and paint normally used for painting plastic models. Make sure the surface is clean of any wax or dirt before applying the paint, and let it dry for several days before attempting to use wax or protectant over it. Pro detailers would also prep taillights for a show car by turning the screws so that they are all aligned, then cleaning any wax or dirt from the screw slots with a toothpick.

6.23 If your plastic-covered bumper needs more than just cleaning and requires repainting, you must use special flexible paints. It used to be that only body shops could do this, but Plastic-Kote makes a bumper-painting system in spray cans that prepares for final color in four preliminary steps.

One of the rubber areas needing treatment that often is overlooked is weather-stripping, those spongy rubber strips that separate your trunk, doors and windows from the body. There's more to protecting them than just looks; detailing here serves some very practical purposes. For one, those rubber strips, which keep wind-noise and water from getting inside, must remain supple and pliant to do their job, and regular cleaning and protectant can keep them that way. We have also seen cases of serious neglect of weather-stripping where dirt, moisture and other contaminants left a stickiness to the weather-stripping that resulted in the spongy rubber actually being torn when the door or trunk was opened, with a chunk of the body-mounted rubber remaining attached to the

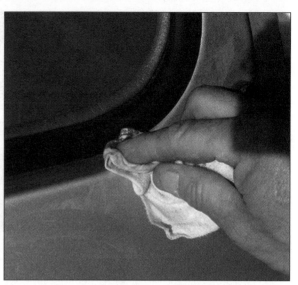

6.24 On close examination, you can see where this weather-stripping at one time stuck to the glass back window of this wagon, causing a tear when the window was opened as the rubber stuck to the glass. Regular treatment with protectant will prevent this.

6.25 Weather-stripping needs an occasional treatment with vinyl dressing to keep it from drying out and deteriorating.

6.26 This vinyl strip above the bumper has been UV faded and has white marks left on it where overzealous waxing caused a wax residue in the grain of the vinyl.

6.27 Protectant is worked into the grain of the black vinyl with an old toothbrush, loosening the wax residue and getting protectant into the pores.

door or trunk **(see illustration)**. Needless to say, the effectiveness of the weather-stripping had been compromised. Given occasional cleaning and treatment with protectant around the door and trunk seals, there should never be a problem with sticking weather-strips.

6.28 When allowed to sit a few minutes before being wiped off with a clean rag, the vinyl strip looks new again, giving a nice contrast with the waxed paint and future protection against wax residue.

6.29 Brushes are very important in detailing. From the left, here are: plastic-bristled brush for exterior washing, a whisk broom for sweeping carpets, a "detailer's" brush for getting wax residue out and a small detailer's brush.

6.30 One of the myriad uses for small, soft-bristled detailer's brushes is during your wash phase, getting out accumulated dirt where it has collected along trim pieces

6.31 On this car, the exterior door handles have a pebbly, black vinyl coating that has faded due to UV exposure with no protection.

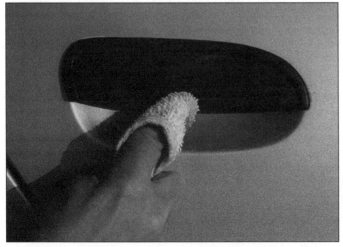

6.32 After the basic carwash, a little application of vinyl protectant on a rag produces dramatic results, turning the handles back to true black instead of gray.

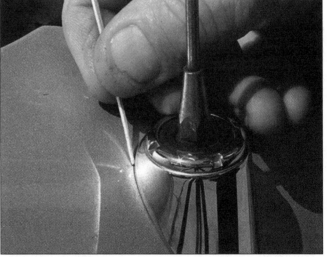

6.33 At car shows and concours events, you'll see plenty of toothpicks in evidence, as they are quite useful for picking out tiny pieces of dirt or wax residue in places like around this antenna trim.

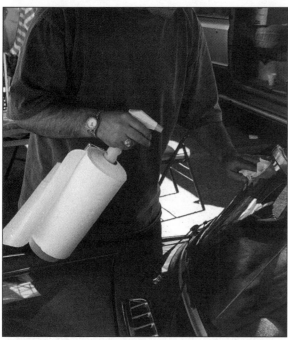

6.34 Light glass cleaning can be done with household glass spray and paper towels. Here a special dispenser (Dazy-Spray) is being used that conveniently holds a roll of paper towels over the thin spray bottle.

6.35 Old-fashioned method of newspaper and vinegar/water solution still does a good job of glass cleaning without leaving lint. Do not get the vinegar/water solution on painted surfaces, though.

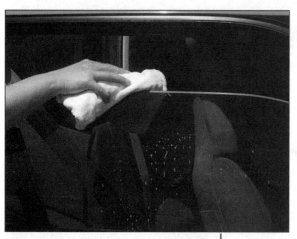

6.36 Side windows should be cleaned along the top edges first with the glass partly rolled down to eliminate dragging this area's dirt (usually the dirtiest spots) around when cleaning the rest of the glass.

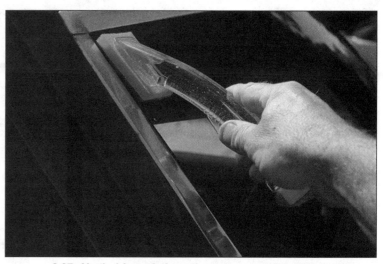

6.37 Alcohol-based glass cleaners are preferred by some detailers and are easily applied without overspray by using an applicator like this which allows you to get right up next to the chrome trim. Use a separate applicator for glass cleaner, not one you have used for protectant.

Glass cleaning

Glass is one of the most durable surfaces on your car, and cleaning it is easy. Lots of weekend detailers use common household spray glass cleaners, and they will work, but the environment of automotive glass is different than that of house windows. There are better products for this situation. The problem with the most common household glass cleaners is streaking, which requires several applications to clear up. Some of the conditions unique to automotive glass are road tar, bug splatters, rock chips, acid rain and hard water spots. Clear vision is important when driving, and, after you have done a good job on the paint and other exterior details, windows that are anything short of spotless really stand out like a sore thumb.

Traditionally, the best home remedy for glass cleaning was a pad of wadded-up newspaper and a solution of vinegar and water **(see illustration)**. This is still a good method, provided the newspaper you're using doesn't use water-based inks. If you get ink-smearing when using newspaper to clean windows, with any cleaning solution, then that paper is using new, environmentally-correct water-based inks. Lots of people use paper towels for glass cleaning, but the static you build up in cleaning the glass and getting rid of spots can make the paper towel lint hard to get rid of. Your best bet, as in other detailing procedures, is to use cotton toweling for glass cleaning.

Your automotive supply store or chain outlet should have a variety of windshield and glass cleaners to choose from. Some feature ammonia, some contain polish and some are alcohol-based. Detailers all have their own personal favorites. The alcohol-based cleaners work well and can be applied with a liquid applicator which eliminates the overspray from spray bottles. You don't want to get glass cleaner on your freshly prepped paint, so the best advice if you're using a spray is to spray it on your sponge or towel first, then applying to the glass. Some people prefer to use plain water first, or water with a tiny bit of car-washing soap in it, then finishing with glass cleaner. Any kind of soap can leave a filmy residue on glass, which will require more cleaning to remove. This is not a problem, according to some detailers, if you mix a small amount of household ammonia (a good grease-cutter) in your bucket of windshield washwater. If you have done a thorough job in your overall washing of the vehicle, most of the dirt and bug splatters will already be gone when you get to final glass cleaning anyway.

When your are cleaning your windows, keep looking at the face of your cloth or sponge. If you see evidence of heavy dirt, it's probably coming from the edges of the glass, where dirt collects next to the rubber molding or gasket. These areas should be cleaned with soap and water and a toothbrush to dislodge dried-on dirt before the final window cleaning; otherwise, you will keep dragging dirt from the corners around with your cleaning cloth and depositing it on the clean areas in the middle.

Back windows are especially hard to clean because you have to lean across what is usually the widest part of body. Make sure you do not wear a belt or have buttons or rivets on your pants or shirt when detailing, they can cause scratches against the quarter panels when reaching across to clean the roof or rear window.

It's important when cleaning door windows that you begin by rolling the window down a few inches and cleaning the top of the glass first, this is an area that is easy to overlook. Do the tops of the windows, then move on to another area of glass to clean. Go back when the tops of the windows are dry, roll them back up and detail the rest.

Several of the leading detailing-supply companies make their own glass cleaners and polishes. They include chemicals and a very fine abrasive to remove tar, bugs and road film. These products are excellent for removing hard-water spots. When hard water (with high mineral content) is left to dry on a hot window, the evaporation leaves behind a stubborn ring of mineral deposits that won't come off with standard glass cleaners. Polish is required to remove these spots. Most good glass polishes are applied much like wax by squirting some on a damp pad and wiping on a thin coat. When it hazes over, buff off with a clean cloth.

Many detailers also keep in their kit some 0000 (4-0) steel wool, which they use carefully to remove stubborn spots from glass, or for removing unwanted stickers and decals **(see illustration)**. We caution against using even such fine grade steel wool on glass because of the chance of inducing scratches. Most

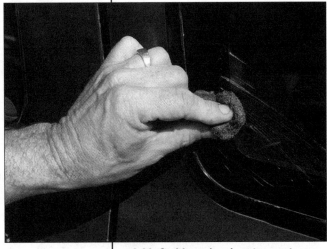

6.38 Stubborn hard-water spots can be removed from glass with fine steel wool soaked in glass cleaner.

problems can be dealt with by using glass polish, and decals or stickers are best removed with solvents.

Detailing windshields to look their best may involve treating cracks, pits, scratches or stone chips. Some automotive glass shops do glass repairs, consisting of polishing with rouge to reduce the visibility of scratches, or using an injected epoxy resin to "clear" a stone chip. The efficacy of the former process depends on the depth of the scratch and the skill of the glass man wielding the polisher. Some scratches are too deep to repair, and a poor job will only make a larger area of blurry distraction than you had with the scratch.

The repairing of nicks or stone chips may or may not be successful. Anyone can buy one of several "kits" to do this and set themselves up doing mobile glass repairs, but they do not always do a proper job. Your best bet is with a reputable automotive glass shop. The problem with some of these repair kits is that the injected material doesn't cure as clear as the glass around it, although we have seen some that work fairly well. Such repairs can be worth a try, but generally this is a stall tactic to avoid buying a new windshield.

In areas of the country where there is a lot of rainfall, you can try a product called Rain-X. This has been around for many years and is well known to owners of sports and specialty cars. Recently it has become more widely available for the general consumer in automotive supply or chain stores. You apply this clear product to a clean windshield or outside mirror, let it haze and then buff it off. It leaves a polymer coating on the glass that actually repels water. In cases of light rain where using the wipers is overkill, the water will bead up and then run off the treated windshield. At highway speeds, the air hitting the windshield may be enough to carry all the water off without using your wipers. It's not a substitute for having wipers, but some motorists carry a bottle in the glove box in case they get caught in a storm and find their wiper motor has quit or their blades are shot. It's excellent for keeping a clearer view in outside mirrors.

Convertible and vinyl tops

Convertibles are fun cars to drive, especially on summer days with the top down, but you have to "pay for your fun" in the sense that convertibles require

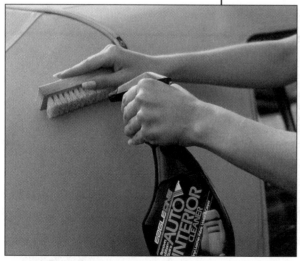

6.39 Standard vinyl convertible tops can be easily cleaned with vinyl interior cleaners if the top isn't too dirty. Using a scrub brush, work it into the grain of the vinyl; then rinse off with clean water and towel dry in the shade.

6.40 Besides the vinyl top itself, most convertibles also have a boot cover that should receive the same cleaning and protection as the top and other areas. This vinyl boot can be cleaned with standard products. Some high-end cars have a painted metal boot that should be cleaned and waxed along with the exterior paint.

6.41 The cloth top on this vintage car hasn't been given the same attention as the remarkably-preserved paint job. Stains and general discoloration can be addressed with the proper cleaning methods to fend off the expensive-but-inevitable top replacement.

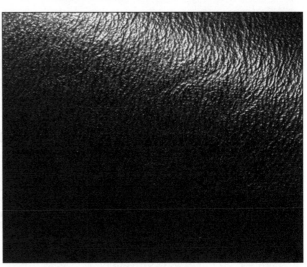

6.42 Exterior vinyl material has a deep grain molded in to simulate the appearance of leather. Unfortunately, this grain tends to catch and hold dirt unless it is cleaned and kept protected.

extra work detailing, particularly their tops. Driving with the top down also means interior cleaning will be a little tougher, with more dirt and airborne pollution getting on your seats and panels. All that extra sunshine on your interior also means you must use protectants on the interior to prevent fading and cracking of your leather or vinyl.

There are two types of convertible top material. Most cars have a vinyl-coated canvas cloth, which is also found on padded vinyl tops, but some high-end European cars and classic cars have real cloth tops which require special consideration when cleaning **(see illustration)**.

The problem with cleaning a vinyl/cloth convertible top is that, due to the heavily-grained texture of the material, a scrub brush and sometimes

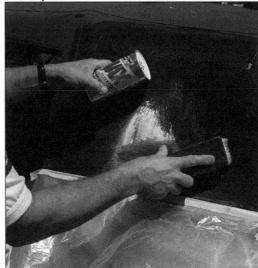

6.43 Deep cleaning of stains or discoloration on convertible tops may require strong household powdered cleanser used in a "slurry" paste with water and an SOS pad or scrub brush. The surrounding paint should be protected with masking.

6.44 High-end luxury and sports cars often have genuine cloth tops which look elegant but are more susceptible to deterioration from the elements and should never be cleaned or treated with vinyl products.

6.45 With a cloth top, wet down during your basic washing treatment, sponge the top with suds from a dedicated car-washing soap only. Using a soft sponge or mitt, gently go over the plastic back window at the same time.

6.46 The grain of the cloth can be scrubbed if necessary with a brush to work out any dirt.

6.48 Remove the excess rinse water from the cloth material with lint-free cotton towels, but leave the plastic window alone at this time.

6.47 Hose the top assembly thoroughly to rinse any trace of the soap from the cloth top material and the back window.

tough cleaning agents are needed to get them really clean **(see illustrations)**. You don't want to get these cleaning products on your paint because they can strip off your wax protection and may even streak your paint. When faced with a convertible top that has been neglected and needs serious cleaning to get it to our "baseline" stage of preparation, pro detailers often mask off the surrounding areas of the car body with masking tape and plastic sheeting **(see illustration)**. This is just for insurance and won't be necessary every time you clean the top. Once you have the top material as clean as you can get it, treat it with vinyl protectant and it will clean up very easily thereafter.

Many convertible tops are white or buff colored and when neglected become brown with accumulated dirt and stains. Sometimes to get one clean and bright again you have to use strong cleanser with bleach, such as household powders like Ajax or Comet. Wet the top surface down, sprinkle on some cleanser and rub it in with a scrub brush in a circular motion, alternating the direction of your cir-

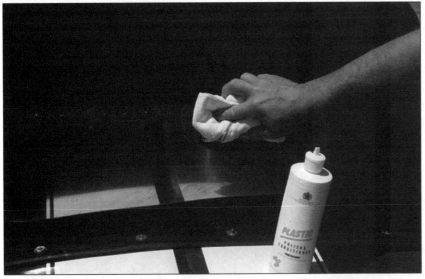

6.49 Few areas of a car are as fragile as the plastic rear window in a convertible, but they can be kept looking very new with frequent polishing with dedicated plastic polish. Most brands suggest considerable shaking of the contents before applying the milky plastic polish, which has tiny abrasives in suspension.

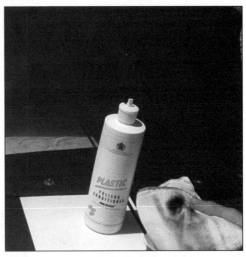

6.50 A neglected window may take several applications to come sparkling clean. Use only a very soft cloth like diaper material, and turn the cloth over frequently. Even a window that appears clean can deposit dirt as shown on your cloth. You don't want to drag that dirt around, scratching the rest of the window.

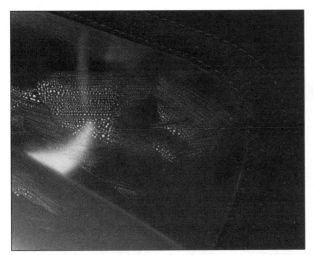

6.51 For the last application of plastic polish, apply liberally and let it dry to a haze evenly across the window. It will be easy to see the areas not covered.

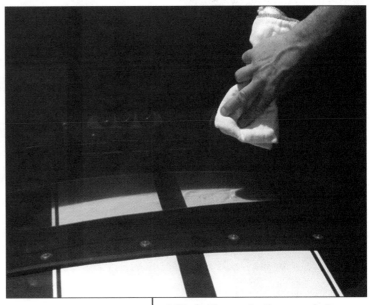

6.52 Getting a plastic rear window clean means doing the inside and outside several times, but the final wipeoff with a clean cloth restores the window to almost-new visibility and appearance.

cles now and then. Rinse each section as you finish it, without waiting until the whole top is done. Use plenty of rinse water to remove any abrasive particles left from the powdered cleanser. When using such household cleansers, you must mask off the rest of the body. We recommend not using a high-pressure spray for rinsing, such as at a coin-op car wash, because the pressure can force the residue of the cleansers down into seams in the top and where the top meets the body. After a serious cleaning like this, immediate protection of the vinyl material is very important, because you have stripped the top of its gloss and protection. There are several protectants on the market that are just for convertible tops, but most interior vinyl protectants will do the job. Just let it sit on the (shaded) surface of the material for a minute or two before buffing it off, letting it penetrate.

6.53 If you have a sunroof, open it up after your basic carwash. Get a rag dampened with soapy water or Simple Green and clean all around the edges of the body opening and the sliding tracks.

6.54 A detailer's swab is being used here to apply rubber protectant to the sealing edge of this sunroof, maintaining the sunroof's watertightness.

If these methods don't provide a satisfactory result with your top, you probably need a new top, and, knowing what you know now, you'll probably take much better care of the new top than you did the old one. Actually, the last choice before having a new top installed would be to refinish or paint the old top. If it's still in good condition, meaning the threads aren't coming out of the seams and there aren't holes in the material, then the top can be painted to prolong its life a little longer. Special paints are made for convertible and vinyl tops, available in either spray cans or in bulk for use with a regular automotive spray gun as used in shops. If you are repainting it, you can, of course, opt for a different color if you like, but more coats will be required to cover the old color. You need to do a very careful job of masking off the rest of the car when respraying a top, and it's best to do it indoors where wind won't be factor. Also, whether you are changing the color or not, it is better to do several light coats of paint rather than one heavy one. Not only will you avoid drips, runs and uneven color, but heavy coats could bleed through the top material to the inside if you're not careful.

Most convertible tops don't need such extreme treatments to get them clean. Wash the top right along with the rest of the car with carwash soap, doing the top first and using a soft-bristled brush. Use care not to run the brush onto your painted surfaces - even a plastic supermarket brush can scratch your paint. After the basic washing and drying, use a vinyl cleaner on the top, then treat with protectant. Many of the vinyl top protectants on the market call themselves top "dressing."

Make sure when you do your waxing of the body that you don't get polishes, glazes or wax onto the top material. You may want to mask off the bottom edges

6.55 Here a single-edge razor is being used to trim away excess sealant that has oozed out from under window trim on this camper shell. After this, the area can be polished and waxed right up to the trim for a neater edge. It's little things that add up to a total look that says "detailed."

6.56 Did you forget the door jambs during your car wash? Use a small soapy sponge to clean them, then towel dry. In this case, the interior door panel included delicate suede leather, which was lightly masked off with masking tape so dirty water and soap didn't get on the leather.

of the top when waxing the rest of the body, just to be sure. Be especially careful when operating a buffer near the area where the cloth top meets the body.

The high-end European cars and classics that have real canvas or cloth convertible tops require special care **(see illustration)**. The material is sensitive and very expensive to replace! Some custom shops also use such material in making "faux" convertible tops, by gluing it over the car's hardtop and making the back window smaller to look more like a true convertible. Some detailers use fabric upholstery cleaners on this kind of material, but check your owner's manual before trying them if your car is still under warranty. The kindly man at the BMW or Mercedes dealer will be happy to sell you some of their own factory top cleaning products, but be prepared - the cost of the factory cleaners is commensurate with the cost of the cars. None of the other vinyl cleaners, dressings or protectants we have mentioned should be used on these true cloth tops.

The last detail unique to convertible tops is the plastic rear window, perhaps the most fragile surface on the car. Even a household sponge can be abrasive enough to scratch a plastic window. Use only soft cotton cloth, like well-washed T-shirt material, to wash or clean plastic rear windows **(see illustrations)**. After basic washing and drying, use a plastic cleaner to remove any water spots, stains or scratches from the plastic; then use a new clean cloth to apply plastic polish. Using care and continued detailing, the plastic window can last as long as the rest of the top. The number of convertibles you see on the road with tops that are decent but have hazy, cracked or obscured rear windows just goes to show how many people don't know about, or have time for, proper detailing. The other extreme can be found at car shows and concours events where originality is very important in judging and where you see lots of older cars with original tops that look virtually new because the owners took the time to preserve them.

Notes

7

Paint repairs

7 Paint repairs

Rare is the car on the road today that doesn't exhibit at least a few scratches or chips in its paint, even if it has very little mileage on it. Sooner or later, fate and nature will have their way, and your pride-and-joy will be subject to rocks flung up by a truck ahead of you, a toy missile from one of the neighborhood kids will target your car, a runaway shopping cart at the grocery store will scrape the side of your truck or a nasty vandal will purposely scratch your fender with a car key. All of these terrible fates happen to nice paint jobs every day, but, thankfully, anything that can be damaged can usually be repaired.

We're concentrating here on very simple repair treatments for minor scratches and chips as part of an overall auto detailing program. For much more detailed information on serious body cosmetics, see the Haynes "Automotive Body Repair & Painting Manual."

What method you use to repair or conceal chips and scratches will depend on the effort you're willing to put into it. If you have a lot of chips and scratches, you'll have to determine where the repair efforts aren't worth it and whether the panel or the whole car needs repainting. For a few minor chips as most cars are likely to have, they can be repaired/concealed to appear about 75% less noticeable with the most basic approach to touch-up.

The time-honored and simplest way to deal with scratches and chips is to simply apply drops of factory touch-up paint and leave it at that. Most touch-up paint bottles have an applicator inside (like a nail-polish brush), or you can use the end of a paper match or a toothpick to apply it. The latter works best in applying only a tiny amount if necessary. The factory brush in the jar puts on way too much paint so that it usually makes a small chip end up looking a lot bigger. If you can't find the color you need for your car in a touch-up bottle, check your auto parts store in the spray-paint racks. There is a much wider selection of "original" touch-up paint colors in spray cans than in little bottles. To use the spray paint just like regular touch-up paint, shake the paint well and spray it into a small paper cup, or even the plastic top to the spray can. You can now dip into that collected liquid paint with your toothpick or paper match.

One of the problems with most amateur applications of touch-up paint is that they don't get the original scratch or chip clean enough before they apply the paint, leading to early failure of the repair. You should obtain some "wax-and-grease-remover" at your auto paint store and use it to thoroughly clean the depth of the chip or scratch.

The touch-up paint method makes the chip much less visible, as well as protects the body from rust in that spot, but the chip or scratch rarely blends in well with the surrounding paint. It may not be the same color exactly and probably isn't the same height as the paint around it. This is close enough for the average motorist but seldom good enough for a high-end vehicle or a concerned detailer. We illustrate here a method of repair using a "Chip Kit" which has all the supplies you need for a quality touch-up except the actual color to match your vehicle .

Many minor scrapes and shallow scratches can be eliminated or reduced with nothing more than wax and polishes **(see illustrations)**. Try this first before doing anything more drastic. If that doesn't work, then clean the chip thoroughly with a special fiberglass-bristled brush; then color it with your touch-up paint. When this has dried for several days, apply the clear lacquer to the repaired area until the surface is built up to slightly higher than the paint around it. When that is dry, it can be brought down to a level surface with the supplied ultrafine sandpaper, then polished and blended in with paint polish and finally waxed for protection.

Professional detail shops and some body shops offer airbrush touch-up service for scratches and chips. A good airbrusher can mix a perfect match to your color and spray tiny amounts into the damaged area, which can be polished later and glazed and waxed. The thin paint used in the airbrushing will not fill in the scratch to be level with the rest of the paint, but the quality of the color-match makes most repairs nearly invisible.

7.1 This is typical of parking-lot damage, a scrape that could have come from a shopping cart or a careless person parking next to you and opening their door into your paint. Before repainting it, try rubbing compound.

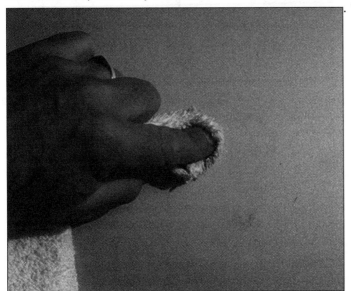

7.2 Rubbing compound and a terrycloth towel are rubbed vigorously onto the scratch until most of the damage miraculously disappears.

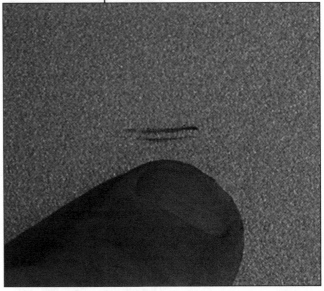

7.3 After polishing and waxing, all that remains of the original damage is this tiny scratch, obviously the deepest part of the damage. You may decide to leave the damage at that, or pursue touch-up work to conceal what remains.

7.4 Pro Motorcar Products markets this paint thickness gauge, which can be useful in determining how thick your paint actually is before doing any buffing or other paint repairs. If the paint is too thin, repairs may cut through to your primer, at which point the panel will need complete repainting.

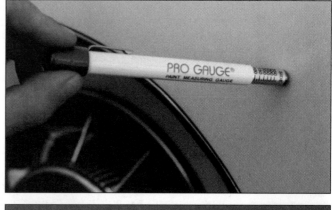

7.5 Also from Pro Motorcar is this handy Chip Kit, which contains all you need to fix and blend in a chip or scratch except the actual touch-up color for your car which you get at your car dealer or auto supply store.

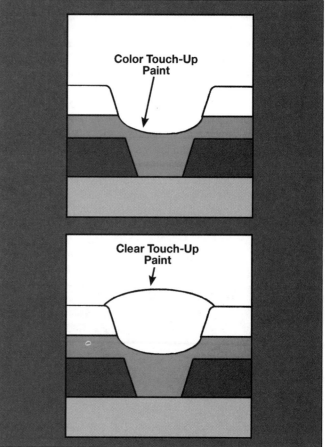

7.6 Under great magnification, your paint damage looks like a crater or ravine. The most invisible repair means coloring that crater, then bringing it up to above surface level with clear, protective lacquer.

7.7 Basic touch-up paint available from auto parts stores should be a close match to your car's paint, but due to the myriad colors and shades that come out each year, it can sometimes be difficult to find touch-up paint for more than a few years back. It is suggested that you buy a bottle or two when you buy your new car and keep them in the glove box for future use.

7.8 If a better match for your paint is available only in a spray can, aim the spray into the cup from the top of the can and then use that liquid paint for touch-ups with a paper match or toothpick for an applicator.

7.9 The Pro Motorcar "Eliminator" is a glass fiber rust removing brush that scrubs the bottom of a chip to clean it and provide a good "tooth" for the paint to adhere to.

7.10 Use a standard touch-up applicator or a paper match to deposit the touch-up color into the cleaned-out chip.

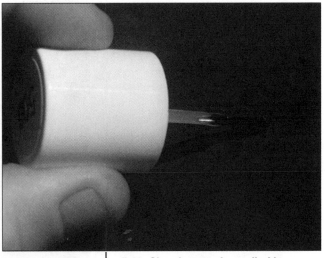

7.11 Clear lacquer is applied in several coats after the original color paint has thoroughly dried, which usually takes several days.

7.12 When the repair is built up to slightly above the surrounding paint, the area is sanded flat with several grades of ultra-fine sandpaper wrapped around a soft rubber sanding block.

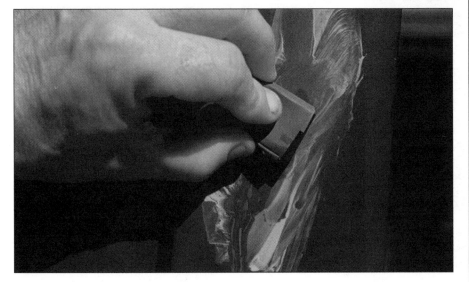

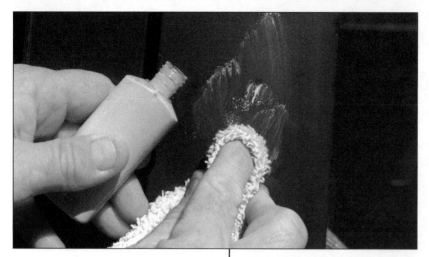

7.13 Very fine polishing compound is then used to blend the repair and sanded area into the rest of the paint.

7.14 The repaired area can now be waxed for gloss and protection, providing a near-invisible repair of chips and scratches.

7.15 The pro detailer offers airbrush touch-up work in his shop, using a bank of small color bottles to come up with a custom-mixed sample amount of paint that exactly matches the subject car's original paint color. Even custom paints and colors that have faded can be matched with this method.

7.16 Up on the counter here at left is the small compressor used to power the professional airbrush gun. Plenty of lighting is required to make close color-matches and apply the paint correctly.

7.17 After all the scratches and chips on the car have been located and cleaned with wax-and-grease remover, the detailer moves his head from side to side until the reflections of his overhead lights show up the nicks and chips perfectly. He applies enough color to fully disguise the defect, with a little overspray around it for blending.

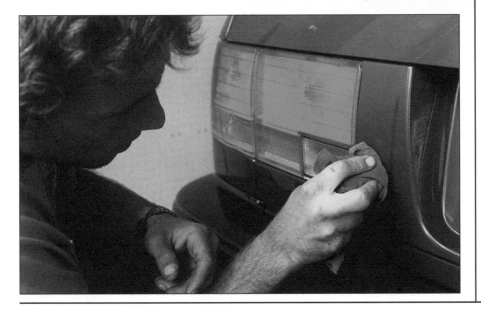

7.18 After the paint has dried (a half hour), the spotted-in areas can be hand polished with very fine compound, and this is where the real expertise comes in. It takes a good eye and an experienced hand to blend the repair in with the least amount of polishing. Polish just a little too hard and the new paint comes out of the scratch and you must start over again. Check your Yellow Pages for someone in your area who offers airbrush touch-up work.

Notes

8

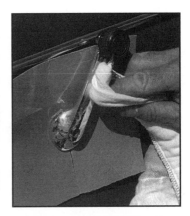

Interior detailing

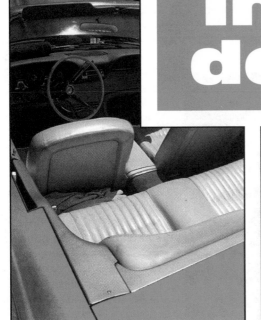

8 Interior detailing

Although a car's interior is rarely as exposed to the harshness of the elements as the exterior of the body, the interior does have its own share of wear factors that ultimately affect the longevity of its looks, comfort and, of course, the resale value of the car.

Every time we climb in and out of the car, we bring in dirt and atmospheric pollution with us. Our shoes carry mud, glass chips, grass clippings, snow, water, old gum and other materials into the car where they can be ground into the carpeting. Such detritus may also become dried while we are driving and then is free to float around the interior and settle everywhere. Sometimes it's amazing how quickly dust accumulates in our vehicle's interior. Take a damp tissue once a week to the top of your dash and just see what it picks up; you'll be stunned at how much dust there is, even if you pride yourself on keeping your car clean.

Drivers who smoke create their own set of problems for the interior. The smoke settles into everything - headliner, carpets, seats, dash and the interior glass. The brownish haze on interiors windows is usually associated with smokers, but non-smokers who haven't kept up with their detailing are always shocked to find a similar film inside their cars. The problem is that all those plastic elements of the interior, including the carpeting, upholstery, dash and all the

8.1 Maintaining the appearances of your car's interior can really enhance your driving pleasure and pride in the vehicle, since all of your driving is done from there. After the exterior paint, the interior is the next most important area to keep clean and the second easiest to get dirty.

trim, emit solvents that slowly and continually evaporate from the vinyl. This film is most noticeable on the glass, and just as difficult to remove as smoke film, but it does settle on everything else as well. Although the accumulation of dirt and filmy haze in the interior tends to sneak up on you more subtly than the obvious dirt on the exterior paint job, vigilance in keeping the interior cleaned and protected is no less important than cleaning and protecting the exterior.

Vacuuming

Most people vacuum the carpeting in their home at least once a week, and allergy sufferers may vacuum even more frequently. The carpeting in your car deserves attention at least as often,

8.2 The powerful vacuum at the coin-operated carwash is excellent for cleaning upholstery and carpeting or even for shampooing your interior. Be ready before you drop your quarters in by removing packages, papers and floormats from the interior before you start.

given that the car's carpeting is subjected to so much more abuse. There is no "welcome mat" outside your car that you wipe your feet on every time you enter as you would in a home, and the dirt tracked in, and the wear from your feet, packages, etc., is concentrated in a very small area. It's as if you never wiped your feet before you came in the house and spent all your time walking on an area of carpet no bigger than 10 or 20 square feet! As any carpet salesman or rug-shampoo operator can tell you, frequent vacuuming is the key element in making carpeting last. When dirt is left in carpeting, it works its way down into the nap, and the friction of walking on the carpet tends to grind the dirt in, wearing the fibers out prematurely, as well as making the dirt much harder to shampoo out.

A detailed interior that is vacuumed frequently can probably be maintained using a simple home vacuum cleaner if it's the canister type with a hose and various attachments (preferably plastic). You'll find the crevice tool particularly helpful. Getting to an initial baseline with the interior will probably require a heavy-duty vacuum such as found at the local coin-op car wash. It may take a few dollars worth of quarters to get it clean the first time, even more if you are going to shampoo the carpeting and upholstery. For minor cleanups on a frequent basis, there are 12-volt car vacuums that plug right into your cigarette lighter socket, and which work fine for picking up dust, snack crumbs, etc. They lack the power to do deep cleaning but are a handy item to carry with you in the trunk along with your other detailing supplies.

When using the coin-op carwash's vacuum, time is money, so be prepared before you start the machine. Remove the floor mats and any packages or other objects that are on the floor or seats. Clean off any papers from the top of your dash and rear package shelf. If you have a center console, take everything off the top. If you have "map" pockets in your door panels, remove all the papers, maps, pens and anything else that has accumulated there, and, if your vehicle has one of those "open" doorless glove box areas, empty it, too. Any items hanging from your rearview mirror should be removed, and mementos or hanging air fresheners should be removed from the dash area, or they could be sucked up in the powerful vacuum action.

Carpeting that is really neglected should be brushed with a stiff whisk broom or brush before you begin vacuuming to help loosen up dirt that may be imbed-

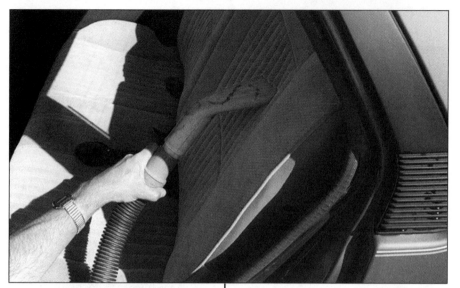

8.3 The crevice tool usually found on coin-op carwash vacuums is ideal for most carpet and upholstery chores, allowing you to really reach into folds of material and between the upper and lower seat cushions.

ded so the vacuum picks it up easier. Drop your quarters in and begin vacuuming your interior by starting from the top down with the headliner. The headliner is rarely vacuumed by a regular commercial carwash, but it's amazing how much dust can be collected there. If there are ribs in the headliner, make sure you press the vacuum nozzle into all the crevices of the seams, and where the headliner ends meets the body all the way around. There is usually a trim band there that can collect dust easily. If you are using your own home vacuum, put the attachment on that has a small brush around it - this will work well for cleaning the headliner, dash and door panels. Brush the dash with your whisk broom and immediately vacuum it to remove loosened dust; then go around the window trim, front, back and sides, and proceed to the door panels. On door panels, pay particular attention to the places where dust collects easiest: around seams, moldings, armrests, handles and even speakers.

Vacuum the seats next, getting the nozzle into all the creases and seams of the material, whether vinyl, leather or cloth, and make sure you flip front seatbacks forward to get into that hiding spot under the seat back. Some detailers will actually remove the back seat cushions to clean around them thoroughly (this also makes shampooing the rear seat a lot easier than doing it in place with you hunched over the cushions. You may even find a few extra quarters back under there. After cleaning the seats, finish vacuuming by doing the carpeting, and spend plenty of time here, forcing the nozzle back and forth through the nap, getting all the little "nits" stuck in the carpeting. Move the front seats forward and back on their tracks to get at all the carpeting underneath, and even vacuum the tracks which tend to attract dirt and debris due to the lubricant used on the slides.

Carpet cleaning

If you have done your vacuuming at the coin-op car wash, you can now proceed to shampoo the carpets. Home vacuums aren't recommended for this because they aren't designed to pick up moisture, although if you have a wet/dry vacuum out in your shop or garage it will work fine. If using a standard home vacuum, try to use the foamy aerosol type of carpet cleaner; it really puts a lot less moisture into the carpeting. If you have some serious spots or stains, treat them first with a household carpet spot-cleaner before you shampoo. These products usually work best on dry carpeting. Spray the stained area, scrub the cleaner in with a stiff brush, let the cleaner dry to a whitish residue, then vacuum vigorously. If this doesn't remove the problem, you may need professional steam-cleaning. You can rent industrial-type carpet cleaning machines at many hardware stores and su-

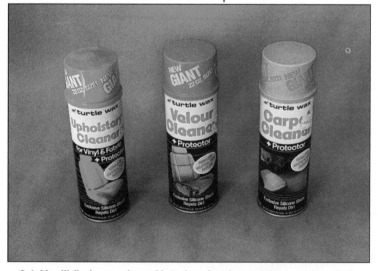

8.4 You'll find a number of interior cleaning products at the chain store or auto parts outlet, like this lineup from Turtle Wax. These will do an excellent job on all but the most soiled carpet and upholstery.

8.5 The next time you or a neighbor clip a carpet coupon from the newspaper and are having the truck-mounted steamcleaners come, ask the gentleman how much more he would charge to do the carpeting in your car, as long as he's there.

permarkets, or have the local carpet-care people do your car's carpeting the next time they're at your house to clean the household carpeting.

If you rent one of the commercial machines, be prepared to spend the day at home because the seats and carpet will take hours, or the better part of a sunny day, to dry after using this kind of soapy-water-and-vacuum equipment. After this kind of treatment, leave your doors open to allow plenty of air circulation so the carpets dry quicker. Most cars have dome and interior lights that come on when you open the doors, so, in order not to run your battery down while you leave your doors open, either place a prop of some kind in the door jamb that keeps the buttons closed or disconnect the battery during the drying process.

After treating any spots, spray your foam-type carpet cleaner on, using a stiff, short-bristled brush to work it into the carpet. If you are working on the front carpeting and you normally have floormats in place, the carpeting may be mashed down quite a bit or even have a transfer pattern to it from the little rubber "bristles" on the backside of the floormats. Carpeting that has been crushed like this for a long time will take vigorous scrubbing to get the nap back up again. After giving the carpet cleaner an appropriate amount of time to loosen the imbedded dirt (follow the recommendations on the bottle or can), you can vacuum the carpets one last time to get all the dirt and cleaner residue out; then just wait for the carpeting to dry. For a really thorough job on carpet that had been neglected in the past, you might do one more vacuuming when everything is dry, to catch any dirt that may have stayed in the carpeting while the fibers were wet.

If you have had a problem with water leaking into the interior in the past, you may have a mildew problem. Left unchecked, it will ruin the carpeting, not to mention leave a depressing odor in your car.

8.6 The steam-cleaning treatment is the best for really getting out ground-in dirt, and the professional operators can do your car's front and back carpets in no time at all.

8.7 Carpeting and upholstery that is subject to a lot of wear and exposure to dirt and stains can be somewhat protected by applying Scotchgard treatment that is available in a spray can.

In such cases, it's best to actually remove or at least pull up the carpeting to take out the padding underneath. The padding may be holding water which keeps feeding the growth of the mildew even though you may have cleaned the carpeting on top. Clean and dry the padding and carpeting, and perhaps spray the padding with a household germ-killer like Lysol spray. Put the padding back in place when dry and put the carpeting back down. To remove or reinstall most carpeting, you have to take off the front kick panels and probably a metal sill molding below the doors. That's a good time to clean the sill moldings (and their screws, which normally get filled with dirt in the slots) while you're at it. The sill moldings are usually anodized aluminum, so use non-abrasive or very mild polish on them; follow with a coat of liquid wax and they're good as new. If there has been evidence of mildew, you should certainly find the source where water has been leaking in and fix it. And if the shampoo treatment didn't eliminate the musty smell of mildew, it's time for new carpeting and perhaps new padding as well. If you install new carpeting, you may want to treat the new material with a protective fabric spray like Scotchgard, which will make the surface much less vulnerable to stains. In fact, such protective measures make good sense for prolonging the life of original carpets, too.

Upholstery cleaning

After a thorough vacuuming of the interior, you can assess the condition of the upholstery. Vinyl can suffer from grime collected in the seams and crevices, or even in the "grain" of the material while cloth seats are much more subject to stains. Cloth upholstery is perhaps the toughest material to clean, especially if there are stains, because the stain goes right into the material, rather than being mostly on top of the surface as with leather or vinyl. Try spray spot removers first on an inconspicuous area around the bottom of the seats to make sure that the product you're trying won't take the color out of your cloth upholstery. If it doesn't, then use that spot remover on any stains or discolorations you may have on the seats. As mentioned above, these kinds of spot cleaners work best on dry material. You spray them on, scrub

8.8 In the One Grand line of detailing products, they offer interior cloth cleaner, leather cleaner and protectant. They are one of the few companies to offer two kinds of vinyl protectant: Do-It-All and ERV. The former is for interior vinyl and doesn't leave an ultra-glossy look on things, while the ERV is for exterior vinyl and lasts longer under outdoor exposure.

8.9 If you don't have a canister-type vacuum at home, regular light vacuuming can be done with either a 12-volt vacuum plugged into the lighter socket or a rechargeable DustBuster like this. Here cloth seats are being vacuumed before upholstery cleaner is used.

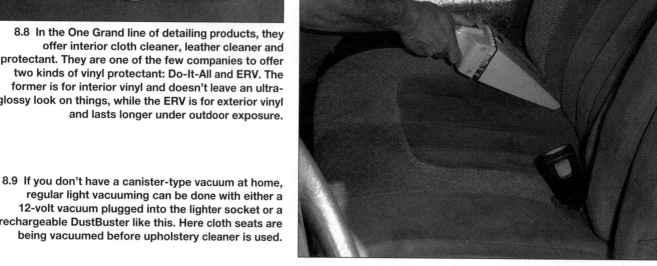

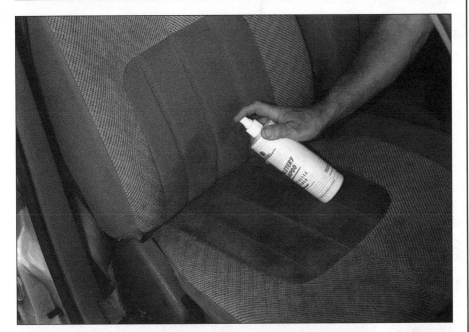

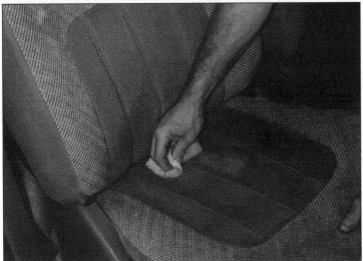

8.10 Upholstery shampoo usually is low in water content to shorten drying time, so don't be surprised if large quantities don't spray out with each pump. Spray the whole seat area with extra squirts where there are stains.

8.11 A wet sponge is used here to scrub the shampoo into the material and loosen up the dirt in the weave.

8.12 Your sponge must be rinsed out constantly in clean water to keep from redepositing dirt on the upholstery as you clean.

in with a short, stiff brush, then let dry to a white, powdery residue which you can vacuum off.

With any stains addressed, you can proceed to shampoo the upholstery. This really helps to unseat (pardon the pun) embedded dirt and give the whole interior a clean, new-smelling atmosphere. It makes sense to clean the back seat area upholstery first, if only so that you don't have to crawl over your just-cleaned-and-still-wet front seats to get to the rear. The foam shampoo should be worked into the fabric with a short brush, and an old toothbrush will come in very handy for getting into small areas like upholstery seams. It helps if you push and pull on the seats to open up the seams and folds while you are brushing the shampoo in. If you don't have any foam upholstery shampoo handy, you can use a sudsy solution of household detergent that is made just for delicate fabrics, such as Woolite Gentle Cycle powder. Mix a small amount in a bucket of warm

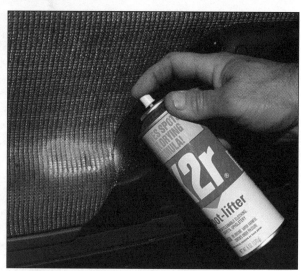

8.13 If you don't have a wet/dry vacuum at home and you're not at the coin-op carwash, use dry, lint-free towels to brush the material, extracting moisture and any remaining dirt. Then let the seats air-dry.

8.14 Household spot removers can do an excellent job of removing stubborn stains from car carpeting and upholstery, provided you test it first on an inconspicuous spot for color-fastness. Texise K2R is being used here to clean the soiled area of this door panel right behind the handle.

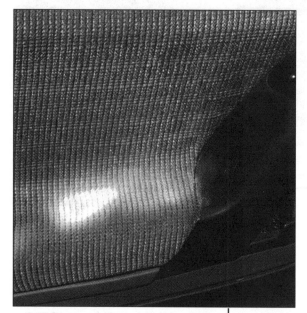

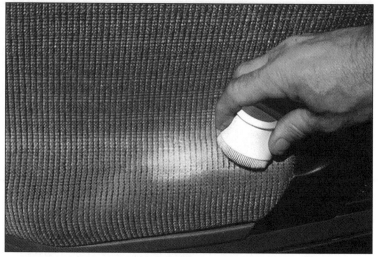

8.16 In this case, the top of the K2R can has a built-in scrubbing brush for removing the powdery residue, but you could also use a small scrub brush.

8.15 Spray only for a second or two, and allow the spot remover to dry thoroughly, usually to a pure white powder.

water, stir it up until there's a frothy head on it and then use mostly the foam part for your upholstery cleaning.

After letting the cleaner work a bit, remove the suds or foam with a clean sponge you rinse out in clear water. It's important to note that any shampoo or soap used on your cloth upholstery should be rinsed out before allowing the material to dry. Obviously, you can't rinse the seats off with a hose, but you can use a sponge in a clean bucket of cool water, and apply only as much rinse water as is necessary to rinse out the suds. To remove the rinse water, you need a powerful wet/dry shopvac or the vacuum at the coin-op carwash. Excess water on cloth upholstery can be blotted off with towels to speed the drying process, and in a pinch, if your need to dry off the driver's seat because your need to drive the car,

8.17 Door panels can be a real mix of surfaces and materials. This Lamborghini door has soft leather, black metal ashtray and wool carpeting at the bottom, and the top features real polished wood trim. This is a car you don't just spray with ArmorAll and wipe down. Each of these surfaces requires its own detailing processes, and one shouldn't slop over onto the neighboring material.

8.18 The grainy nature of vinyl means there are lots of places for dirt to collect, and thorough cleaning requires vinyl cleaner to be working into the surface with a small scrub brush, followed by wiping with a clean cloth and the application of a protectant that is suited to the section you are doing (i.e. not too slippery for seats).

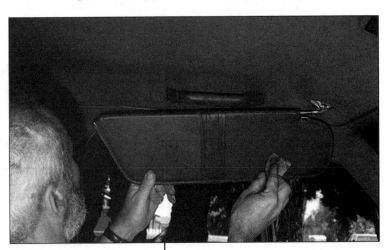

8.19 Protectant is the handiest material ever for cleaning and preserving today's cars, given the amount of plastic and vinyl used now to reduce weight and cost.

you can use a home hair dryer as long as you don't get it too close to the material.

There are some spray fabric cleaners on the market that contain fabric protectant. These are the equivalent of one-step cleaner/waxes for the exterior. They let you do the job quicker and easier, but they won't do as thorough a job as the single-purpose products can do. These spray cleaners wipe off with a sponge or cloth, with no rinsing required (in fact, rinsing could lessen their protectant or stain-repellent qualities).

Vinyl

Vinyl upholstery is much more durable than cloth, is more resistant to stains and can withstand much tougher cleaning methods. Although vinyl can be cleaned effectively with ordinary soap and water and then rinsed, few professional detailers will do this. They prefer to use one of the many vinyl cleaners on the market, either a combination cleaner/protectant or cleaner followed by protectant. Vinyl cleaners should be worked into the material much like the cloth upholstery cleaners, using a circular motion with a brush to get into all the texture of

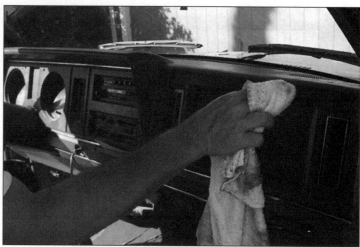

8.21 Protectant livens up and protects dashes, armrests, kick panels, consoles and many other interior surfaces.

8.20 Vinylex is a protectant made by the Lexol leather-care people. It's a good product but one of the only protectants on the market honest enough to say right on the package that it shouldn't be used on seats, steering wheels, pedals or floors because it can make these areas too slippery for safety.

8.22 Vinyl interior parts like dashes, door panels, armrests and even seats can be renewed or have their color changed with vinyl paint dyes. This will not last as long as factory dyed vinyl, but it is inexpensive and easy to use.

the vinyl, and using a toothbrush to scrub in the seams.

Once the cleaner has worked on the vinyl a few minutes, take it off with a clean terrycloth towel, working the towel into all the folds and seams, and anyplace the now-dirty cleaner could have collected. When the vinyl is dry, apply vinyl dressing or protectant, let it soak in a bit, then buff off the excess with a towel. Too much protectant, especially on seats, is improper detailing. Most car enthusiasts can remember years back when ArmorAll first came on the market. It seemed like a miracle product for tires and vinyl, but it had a tendency to leave the surface quite slippery if you didn't buff it off thoroughly. Everyone had their own favorite story about someone who had just treated their car or motorcycle seats with ArmorAll and then drove off, only to find that they were sliding off the seat on corners! ArmorAll has many competitors in the tire and vinyl protectant market today, and ArmorAll even has its own brand of lower-sheen protectant out now (that was another complaint about the original protectants, they left vinyl and tires unnaturally shiny). Today's vinyl protectants do a great job of restoring gloss and oils lost to evaporation, as well as making the vinyl easier to clean in the future.

Use vinyl cleaners and protectants on all your interior vinyl, including the dash, kick panels, moldings on the bottom sides of the seats and vinyl inserts of moldings in the door panels. Let it work in according to the directions; then buff off excess. Most detailers have their own favorite brands they are loyal to. When vinyl is particularly sun-faded, some detailers apply protectant one day, let it sit on the surface overnight for extra protection and then buff off the next day.

A problem that shows up on kick panels is where there are black shoe marks or scrapes - they aren't called kick panels for whimsy. If regular vinyl cleaner won't remove the scuff marks, try some household spray cleaner like 409 or Simple Green, letting the spray sit on the surface for a few minutes to loosen the surface dirt. If that fails to remove all of the scuff, you will have to use an abrasive. Luckily, the color in vinyl or plastic kick panels goes all the way through, so you won't be taking off the original color. Use a plastic polish first or, as a last resort, a household powdered cleanser like Comet, Ajax or Bon Ami. If the cleanser you use has any bleach in it (check the contents), put newspapers or an old towel on the carpeting beneath the kick panel so the cleanser doesn't run off and affect the carpets. After the scuffs are gone, follow with a good coating of protectant.

Leather care

What is different about leather upholstery from the other materials we have described is that it is a natural material, generally the tanned hides of cows or pigs. Because it is a natural animal product, it contains oils that need to be renewed on a regular basis. Without such care, leather will dry up, crack, harden and even start to come off in crumbles. Given that leather upholstery is found only in the most expensive luxury cars, and that it's replacement costs are astronomical, it makes sense to give more detailing attention to preserving leather than any of the other materials we have described. A Mercedes, BMW or Porsche that is in beautiful shape, but has cracked, dry leather will lose thousands of dollars in resale value. After all, the whole appeal of leather in the first place is its natural suppleness. That "new leather" smell in a luxury car or a shoe store smells great, but it's the smell of natural oils evaporating from the leather, an evaporation that will eventually destroy it. Just as a good pair of quality leather shoes can last for many years with proper care, so can your leather upholstery with attentive detailing.

Some leather upholstery materials are coated with a thin plastic "skin" as a protective measure, and those leathers (usually on domestic cars) can be treated much like regular vinyl upholstery, with less frequent detailing than the uncoated kind found in European cars. To find out which kind you have, pull the bottom cushion of the back seat out and test the normally hidden back edge that is normally hidden by applying a drop of water with your fingertip. Observe closely: uncoated "natural" leather will absorb the water; coated leather won't.

While you have the rear cushion out, use that inconspicuous spot at the back to test the leather-care products you intend to use. Make sure that the cleaners or protectants don't change the color of the leather or actually remove the leather's

8.23 Leather interiors require you to take special precautions in care and cleaning, and the suede leather in this limited-edition 84 Pontiac 6000-STE is particularly hard to clean.

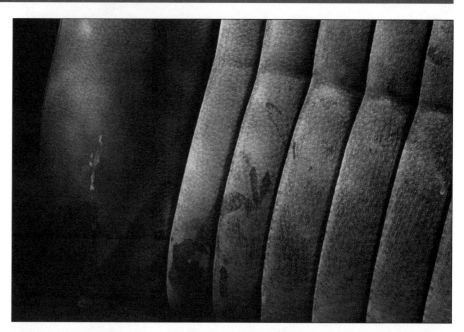

8.24 Stains like this in suede are difficult to remove, and, if you don't have the right materials to treat them, either take the car to an auto upholstery shop for cleaning or find some suede cleaner at the local shoe repair shop.

8.25 This Pontiac had originally come with a suede-pigskin "care package" that contained special suede soap, several brushes and instructions.

8.26 Before applying any cleaners to the suede, brush up the nap of the soft leather with a short-bristled brush. When there is a person sitting on the seat, the fibers get matted down, along with the dirt.

dye. There may be some slight and temporary darkening when applying conditioner to really dry leather, but this is probably closer to the way the leather should really look. Follow the manufacturer's directions closely for the products you use, as procedures vary. Old-fashioned saddlesoap can be used if the leather is particularly dirty, but usually a thorough application of a quality leather cream or liquid conditioner/preserver is all you'll ever need.

Some products specify that you should pre-clean leather with a sponge

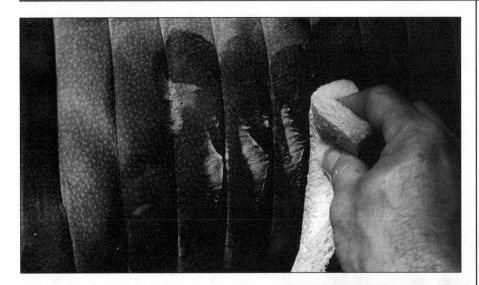

8.27 The special suede soap was applied with a clean sponge and gently worked into a lather. The sponge should be rinsed in clear water frequently. Do not brush the suede while it is wet.

dampened with pH-balanced soap and water, using a short brush (like the kind you car buffs may have at home specifically for cleaning dirty fingernails) to work this into the fold and seams of the leather, spreading the material with your hands to get into all crevices then blotting off with a towel and applying conditioner to restore any oils that may have been scrubbed off the surface. Some leather preservers specify that your should work the product into the leather with your bare hand rather than a cloth. Let it soak in for a half-hour; then buff with a clean terry cloth. Other conditioner manufacturers suggest that their products be applied while the leather is still damp from the cleaning process.

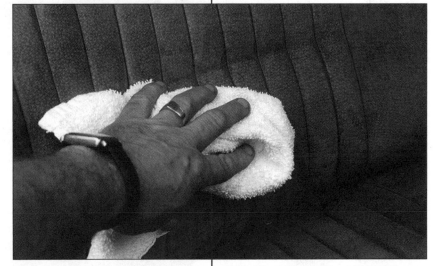

8.28 Rinse the leather with a clean wet sponge; then remove the remaining shampoo residue with a clean, dry cloth.

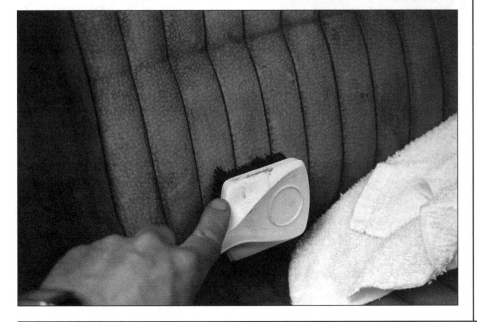

8.29 After the suede has dried completely, raise the nap of the material again with a dry brush, and then vacuum to remove any remaining residue. The suede cleaner is quite diluted, so if one treatment doesn't do it try the process again.

8.30 Lexol is one of the famous names in leather-care products, with both a leather cleaner and a conditioner.

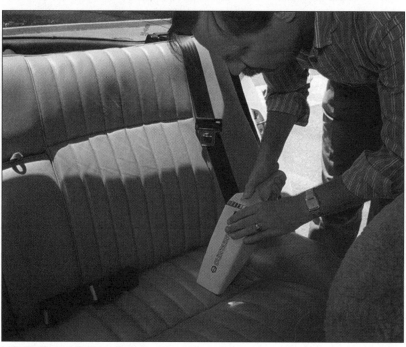

8.31 The seams and crevices of leather upholstery should be thoroughly vacuumed before cleaning or conditioning.

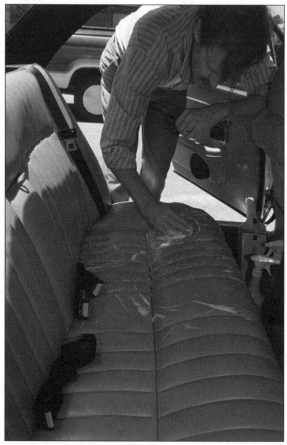

8.32 The liquid Lexol leather cleaner is sprayed on the entire seat bottom of this Jaguar sedan. If there are any cracks in the leather that are light-colored because the cracks go below the surface dye of the hide, the Lexol may slightly darken the cracks; this will eventually fade back in a few days.

8.33 Using a damp cloth, the Lexol cleaner is worked briskly into the leather until a slight lather is brought up on the whole seat bottom.

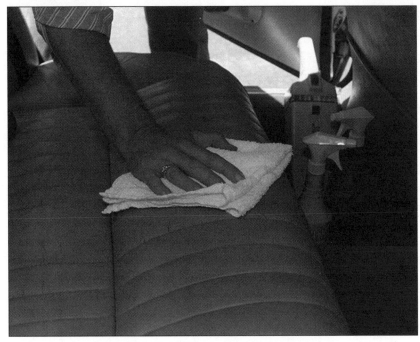

8.34 A clean cloth is used to wipe up the lather and any loose dirt on the surface. Even if you thought the leather was clean before, you'll be surprised at how dirty your cloth can become in buffing off the cleaner.

Manufacturers' recommendations vary as to the amount of time to allow their particular conditioning products to soak into the material before buffing off. If you have cleaned and treated very dry leather upholstery, don't be surprised if the seats seem a bit too shiny even after buffing off the excess conditioner. In a day or two, the surface will settle down to a natural sheen as the conditioner finally soaks all the way into the hide.

8.35 While the seat is still relatively fresh from the cleaning operation, spray on the Lexol leather conditioner and let it soak in for a few minutes.

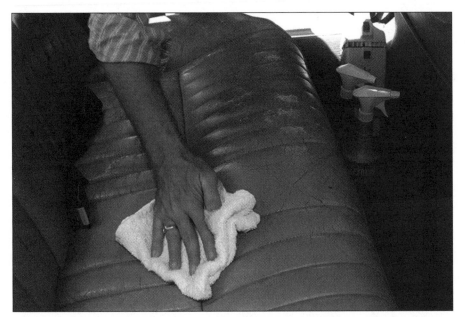

8.36 A second clean cloth is now used to buff in the Lexol conditioner, leaving the leather clean, moisturized and renewed.

8.37 Small applicator swabs like this are available from detailing supply companies like One Grand products. Coated with protectant, they are especially handy for dusting inside crevices and vents. Cotton swabs can also be used.

Small interior details

By now you have gotten the correct impression that detailing means more than just an overall glossing over of major areas, that a well-detailed car exhibits attention to even small matters. Basically, when major areas like your paint, chrome, glass and upholstery are sparkling, it's going to be the little things you skipped that will be most noticeable. Vents, speaker grilles, window handles and even the door jambs require attention to produce the overall impression of a car that has been kept in "like new" condition.

The dash is an area filled with little places to detail. Just dusting with a small cloth and Q-tip swabs moistened with Endust or a similar household product will be a time-consuming but rewarding approach if you really want premium results. The instrument panel should be cleaned with an appropriate cleaner, then treated with protectant, with care taken not to get protectant on the plastic or glass lenses over the gauges until they are first cleaned. These should be dusted first, then cleaned with plastic or glass polish if there are smudges, scratches or discoloration and finally treated with protectant applied with the rolled-up tip of a small, clean cloth.

Make sure that the dash is cool before cleaning or applying protectant. On a hot dash your cleaner will evaporate too fast, leaving dirt streaks everywhere you thought you'd just cleaned.

We have discussed glass cleaning in the previous chapter, but there are two cautions to heed when cleaning interior glass. Of course, you need to roll the windows down a little when starting so that the normally hidden top edge can be cleaned, just as you did on the outside. You don't want window cleaner products on your headliner or other interior surfaces, so apply the cleaner to a cloth first and clean with the cloth rather than spraying cleaner right on the window and taking a chance of leaving unwanted overspray. The other caution is on cars that have aftermarket window tinting (i.e. tint that is applied to the glass, rather than built into the glass as factory tints are). These tints are either applied by spraying a dye on the glass or applying sheets of thin, tinted plastic film to the glass which is the most common aftermarket method. In either case, these tints are fragile coatings and should not be cleaned with harsh cleanser or abrasives. Use only a plastic cleaner that specifies it can be used on interior window tints or that says "non-abrasive" plastic polish. Never use anything with ammonia in it, and only use the softest cotton material like T-shirt cloth, not sponges or paper towels.

Window tinting shops now have special clear plastic films that they apply over the window tint film to provide extra protection. These coverings are said to be more durable than the tint film, and if they do get scratched or stained they can be peeled off and replaced at less expense than replacing the window tint itself.

Your steering wheel takes about as much abuse as any other part of your interior, and, if you are a "car guy" or otherwise work on dirty jobs, chances are your hands have transferred and ground in a considerable amount of grime. Most vinyl cleaners will remove it if you let the cleaner sit there for a while and use some scrubbing action with a nail brush. Clean off the still-wet solution of cleaner and dissolved dirt with paper towels and then apply a second light coat of cleaner to get any remaining deposits. Opinions vary about using standard vinyl protectants on steering wheels. This is definitely an area that can be kept more clean when the material is protected, but many drivers think the protectant makes the steering wheel too slippery for safe driving. If you do use a vinyl protectant or dressing on your steering wheel, make sure you buff off the excess thoroughly, and test the wheel for slipperiness before you get out on the highway. Excess protectant can be cut down with a final, light application of vinyl cleaner.

If you are a smoker, or the previous owner of the used car you just bought was, the ashtrays can become disgustingly coated with hardened, black gook that leaves a permanent smoke odor even long after there has been no actual smoking in the car. Take the ashtrays (some cars have ashtrays in the back seat area as well as in front) out of the car, dump out what you can and soak the inside with Simple Green or Castrol Super-Clean. Really put some cleaner in there and fill the ashtray the rest of the way to the top with water.

8.39 The ashtray can then be soaked in a sudsy bucket for a few hours, then rinsed and dried off. To really do a thorough job of odor elimination, also clean the tracks the ashtray slides on and the area of the dash that is just above the ashtray.

8.38 Dirty ashtrays can contribute to a lingering smell inside a car, even if the current owner doesn't smoke. Serious cleaning with soap-and-water and a short detail brush gets 99% of the gunk out of the ashtray.

8.40 Dashboard and other interior knobs that feature silk-screened text or pictographs should not be cleaned with harsh chemicals. Use soap and water, then protectant.

8.41 Here a worn, high-mileage shift knob has been replaced by the new factory knob. The old knob had become shiny black with all of the vinyl grain worn off. The new one not only looks good, but feels so much better in the driver's hand.

8.42 A cardboard mask is very helpful when you have chrome door handles up against cloth interior panels. When cleaning a chrome handle, the mask protects the upholstery around it. Keep one of these in your trunk for the future.

Leave the ashtray outdoors overnight and then rinse it with a hose. All that junk should come right out. If the there is any stubborn residue left, give it another shot of cleaner and scrape around the wet inside of the ashtray with a flat-bladed screwdriver. Once they are cleaned this thoroughly, including the tracks on which they slide and the outer parts of the tray body, there should be no more odor, leaving the ashtray looking as if it had never been used.

Knobs and handles are next on the interior list. Many of the dash knobs have white or silver lettering indented slightly into the surface (brake release, lights, etc.). When filled with grime and smoke or vinyl emissions, the lettering can be hard to read. Of course, you know what the knobs are for by now, but the dirty lettering is noticeable. Most plastic knobs can be cleaned

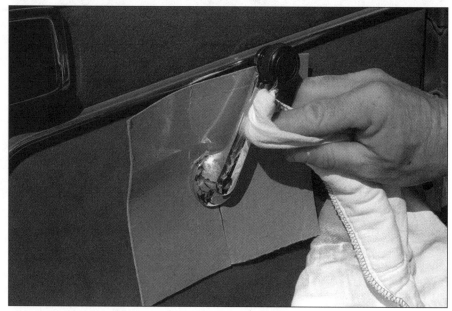

with vinyl cleaner, and, using a nail brush or Q-tip, the lettering can be cleaned out. On knobs where the lettering is simply screen-printed , don't use any abrasive cleaners or the lettering can be scratched right off. Just clean with non-abrasive liquid cleaner and coat with protectant. Door and window handles today use a variety of materials, from chromed metal to plastic chrome and combinations of these with plastic inserts. Use whatever detailing product we have described so far that is appropriate for the material, and don't get extra cleaner or protectant onto neighboring cloth upholstery or on door panels. When scrubbing neglected chrome handles with chrome polish, you can protect the upholstery by using a piece of thin cardboard as a masking shield. Take a piece about five inches square, punch a hole in the center and then cut a path with scissors from the outside of the cardboard to the hole in the middle (see illustration). You can push back the upholstery a little and slide this mask under the handle for protection while cleaning. Keep the cardboard in your detailing kit.

Seat belts are seldom considered in any but the most thorough detailing jobs, but they do get grimy and can be cleaned

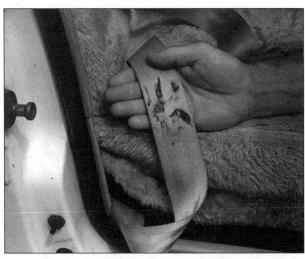

8.43 Soil on seat belts is a common problem, but most people don't bother to clean them. Detailing leaves no area unexamined, so these belts were pulled out of their retractors and found to indeed be dirty.

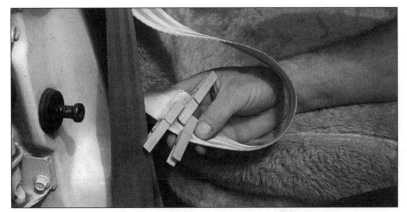

8.44 The seat belt can be kept out for thorough cleaning by clipping on several wooden clothespins to keep the belt out of the retractor.

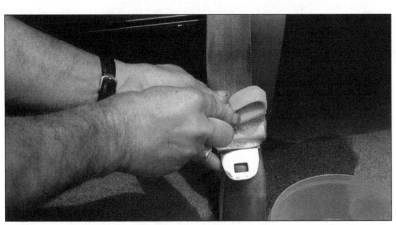

8.45 A fingernail brush and mild vinyl upholstery cleaner can be used to scrub the soiled area of the seat belts. This also works on the buckle and the receptor. Harsh cleaners could fade the color and deteriorate the strength of the stitching.

8.46 The best way to dry the seat belts is to leave them in the sun outside the vehicle after the cleaning treatment.

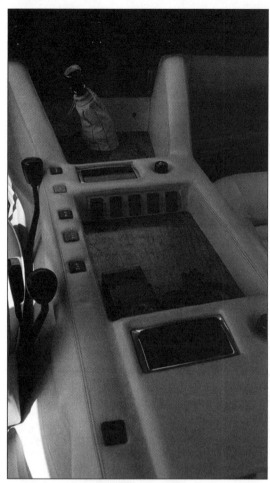

8.47 A variety of surfaces is present on this console, including leather, plastic knobs, metal ashtray, true wood panels and vinyl seat-belt receptacles. Each requires its own procedures without overlap.

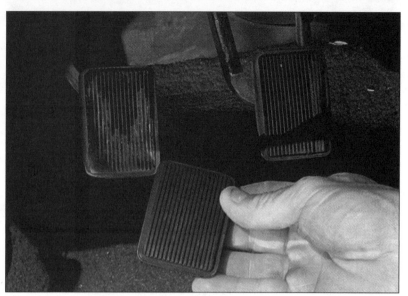

8.48 Worn brake and clutch pedal pads are a sure sign of neglect and high mileage. An inexpensive set of new pads will work better and look better.

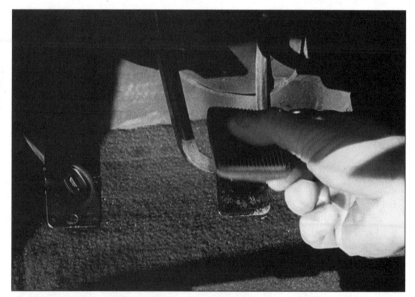

8.49 No tools are necessary to change pedal pads. They just slip on over the metal flange of the pedals. Do not use protectant on pedal pads, clean them with plain soap and water.

with most of the vinyl cleaners we have been using so far. Pull the seat belt as far out of the retractor mechanism as possible, until you see only clean belt coming out, and clip the belt with several clothespins so it will stay out for cleaning. Do not use any ammonia-based products or abrasives here; they could reduce the integrity of the stitching in the seat belts. Use basic vinyl cleaner, wipe off and leave the belts extended until they dry. The metal buckles can be cleaned with chrome cleaner, and the plastic housings the belts come out of, or snap into, can be cleaned with vinyl cleaner and then treated with protectant.

Consoles and glovebox doors are the final chores. On many cars, the glove-

8.50 Whether you consider them part of the exterior cleaning process or the interior process, the door jambs need to be cleaned, first with soap and water, then with cleaner/wax so future dirt has less chance to stick. Note how the suede leather door panel has been protected with masking tape.

8.51 After hand-buffing the cleaner/wax on the door jambs, the tape can be removed. Wax residue could ruin the appearance of the delicate suede.

box door is either painted body color (usually with a dulling agent to reduce glare), or impressed with a vinyl-grain pattern. The latter requires vinyl cleaner with a nail brush to get into all the grain, and the painted doors can be handled with normal cleaner/wax as you would on the exterior paint. If yours is meant to be semi-glossy, don't waste time buffing it to a high gloss or it won't match the painted low-gloss dash around it.

Consoles are another area where detailers have a variety of materials and surfaces. If you have a high-end vehicle, there may be real wood or veneer on the top. If you have a

8.52 Interiors are especially in need of cleaning and protection from UV exposure in convertibles. If you park your convertible for any length of time during the day with the top down, cover your dash with a mat and throw an old T-shirt over each of your front seats for limited protection.

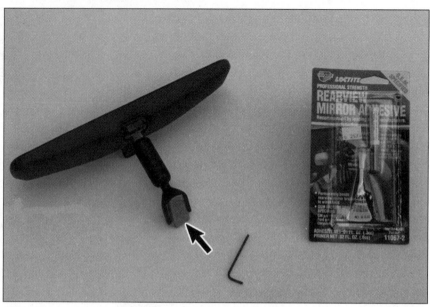

8.54 Even inside rearview mirrors that have fallen off the windshield can be fixed at home, using an adhesive kit from Loctite. The metal mount (arrow) is removed from the mirror, reglued to the windshield and, when dry, the mirror is reattached with the little Allen wrench.

8.53 Don't forget to clean the sunvisors, and when you have the top down check for dirt around the rear top edge of the windshield, the area normally covered by the front header of the top.

van or truck with an aftermarket console, it's probably wood-grained vinyl applied over chipboard, or you may have a console entirely made of plastic, covered with vinyl upholstery material or leather. Using the appropriate cleaner for the surface involved, you will probably have to scrub the recessed areas like a coffee-cup and change holders with a small paintbrush soaked in cleaner. You can make a paintbrush act stiffer by "choking up" on it, applying duct tape over all but the bottom 1/2-inch of the bristles.

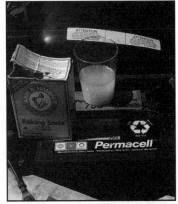

9

Engine detailing

9 Engine detailing

9.1 Anything to do with automobiles can be carried to extremes. We're not suggesting you make your Honda Civic engine look like this, but this enthusiast's obvious love for engines, cleanliness and showy style have resulted in an admirable vehicle that is a strong source of personal pride. Just a little of this dedication will give you satisfaction on your own project.

To those motorists who open their hood only when smoke or steam is escaping, the idea of detailing under the hood may seem like carrying things a bit too far, but we're intent on showing you all of the processes in a total vehicle detailing. You have to decide how far you carry it for your own needs. Before you decide that the engine compartment is one area that you can skip, let's look at engine detailing from a strictly practical standpoint.

First, a clean engine is one that is much easier to maintain when more than a few miles have clicked through the odometer. An engine coated with grease may tend to run hotter than a clean engine, and, when clean, moving parts like linkages tend to work much smoother. Also, battery connections need to be cleaned on a regular basis, or one day you'll hear that dreaded "click-click" that means you are not playing with a full 12 volts.

After 20,000 or 30,000 miles, every engine has the potential for a variety of leaks, such as water, oil, power-steering fluid and transmission fluid (nothing to do with the engine, but the transmission cooling lines run through the engine compartment to the bottom of the radiator). Most maintenance experts will tell you that any mechanical problem should be addressed as soon as it is noticed, on regular underhood inspections, preferably once a week. On an engine covered with road grime and grease, leaks can be very hard to spot. If spotted at all, they can be difficult to trace to their sources when everything is greasy. A clean, detailed engine and compartment makes leak spotting and sourcing easy by contrast, and when engine work must be done it is a pleasure for you or your mechanic to work on an engine that is clean. In fact, we bet most mechanics will do a better or cleaner job on an engine that they see has been maintained fastidiously. They know they're dealing with a car-owner who takes some pride in his machine.

The other main reasons people detail their engine compartment are to keep up the resale value of their car and to show they take pride in its overall look and condition, everything from bumper to bumper. You may have noticed if you have been shopping at any used-car lot that under the hood of every car is

9.2 The trend in specialty cars in recent years is extreme cleanliness, with a monochromatic scheme, where the engine block and engine compartment are all painted the body color, usually a vivid hue.

9.3 An example of good engine compartment maintenance is this 1972 Chevy Monte Carlo. It has well over 100,000 miles on the clock yet looks only a few years old. Only the valve covers have been repainted here; everything else has just been maintained and kept clean.

quite clean and even shiny, as if it were 1000 miles old instead of several years old. It doesn't imply that everyone who turns in a car to a used-car lot had been meticulous in their underhood maintenance. It means instead that car dealers know they can get a better market price and an easier sale when the engine is just as detailed as that rubbed and waxed paint job.

Underhood cleanup is not difficult, and no real mechanical knowledge is necessary (although extensive detailing can involve removing and painting various engine parts and accessories, if you carry the process all the way). You can do it at home in the driveway, at a coin-op carwash, or have the engine detailed by a professional the first time, then maintain it yourself with very simple regular cleanups thereafter. If you're a casual detailer, you may only detail what is immediately visible when the hood is open, things like the air cleaner top, battery top and hoses. If you own a specialty collector car, you will probably want to keep that engine and compartment as original and as new-looking as possible, even if you never take it to a concours or show. Then there is the true "motorhead," the enthusiast who simply loves engines. He has lavished perhaps more time, money and accessories on the engine than the outside of the car, and his engine sparkles like a jewel at all times. The enthusiast is never reluctant to open his hood to show off his engine, either. There are a number of stages to which you can take detailing, and underhood detailing is no exception. It doesn't have to be done all at once, either. You can do the basic underhood cleaning and conditioning one time (probably the biggest effort) and then just detail small parts of the engine and compartment as you find time. Eventually, you'll have things looking even better than those quickie-detailed engines you saw at the used-car

9.4 Your auto supply store has a variety of degreasers, most of which are biodegradable today and non-toxic, though you should observe common-sense precautions about eye and skin protection when using any cleaners.

9.5 For a basic cleanup on a daily-driver, 15 minutes time will bring this dirty compartment to a serviceable level.

9.6 For the most basic driveway engine cleanup, start by covering the distributor, coil and carburetor with aluminum foil, plastic baggies or plastic wrap as shown in the next photograph.

lot. It isn't always just for appearances, either. While doing a good engine detailing job, you may discover a number of minor mechanical problems, like a frayed wire, a deteriorated water hose, loose fasteners, a cracked vacuum hose in the emissions system or a worn or cracked belt. Detailing is one good way to ensure that you really give your engine a thorough inspection.

Engine washing

The first step in detailing the underhood area is washing, which can be as simple as squirting soapy water on and around the engine and then rinsing it off, to working with chemical cleaners, to having everything steam-cleaned professionally. In each example the main plan is to rid the engine of grease and accumulated dirt. The method you use will depend on how dirty your engine compartment is and how clean you'd like it to be.

9.7 After wrapping water-vulnerable components tightly as shown, use a spray cleaner on everything, with particular concentration on the greasiest areas, usually around the valve cover and lower edges of the block. If one section dries out, apply more cleaner.

Each method has its advantages and drawbacks.

In a basic wash and detail, a clean engine may need nothing more than a simple soaping up and hosing down. If the dirt buildup is more advanced than what can be removed this simply, stronger measures are called for. Chemical cleaners for degreasing engines are available in your auto parts store, and there are some household cleaners that can also be used effectively. Most oven cleaners will work well on heavy grease deposits on your engine (observe all the cautions on the container, and wear rubber gloves and eye protection when hosing this caustic stuff off), and many household liquid or spray cleaners like 409 or Simple Green will also work in most cases.

9.8 Depending on how dirty the engine may have been, let the cleaner soak in according to the directions and then hose off the grime and cleaner. Get the rinse water down into every area you can get at; then dry important components with a hair dryer or paper towels.

Next up in terms of effectiveness are the engine cleaners from the auto parts store. Gunk is a widely-available brand that has been used for many years, and the newer Castrol SuperClean is also excellent. Some of the automotive engine cleaners are available in both spray and foam, the latter being good at staying in place on vertical surfaces such as timing covers, firewalls and fenderwells. In years past, pros and amateurs alike have used petroleum-based cleaners like solvent and kerosene to degrease engine compartments. They are inexpensive when purchased in gallon bulk, but pose a minor fire hazard when half-empty containers are kept around in your garage. A gallon of kerosene is just one more "hazardous material," and hardly seems worth the risk to keep around unless you have to degrease a lot of engines. The store-bought cleaners work great without the risk. Whatever you do, **never** use gasoline to clean engines or parts. It's simply too flammable and dangerous, and quite deleterious to your health either from breathing the fumes or through skin contact. In fact, all of the cleaners we are discussing should be used only outdoors with adequate ventilation and with rubber gloves on for skin protection.

9.10 At a professional detail shop, you can bring your car in for a thorough engine steam-cleaning. The detailer (wearing shades for eye protection) will let your engine cool down, then spray everything with their house brand of degreaser and let that sit.

9.9 The local coin-operated carwash is a great place to clean your engine, if they let you. The hot water, soap spray and high pressure are great for cleaning an engine you have sprayed with cleaner, and for the quarters you spend, it's a lot cheaper than either renting a pressure-washer or going to a steam-cleaning operation.

In cases where there is heavy grease, it's helpful to have some kind of pressure to help loosen the deposits. You can do the job in your driveway using a pressurized metal spray container filled with liquid cleaner (or a siphon-type solvent gun that uses your air compressor), or you can use the local coin-op carwash. You may want to have your engine steam-cleaned professionally. In the first case, you have the option of either buying a pressure-sprayer that you can "charge" with up to 100psi of air from the corner service station or your own compressor or renting a pressure-washer if you have a particularly big job. Renting the pressure-washer works out well if you have several cars to do or if you get some friends to come by for engine cleaning and they split the cost with you. The local coin-op carwash is an ideal place to detail your engine - there's plenty of pressure, hot water if you want it, and even soapy water to wash off the chemicals before rinsing with clear water - if they will let you. Due to the accumulation of sludge in the drains at the "engine-washing bay" of the coin-op, recent years have seen environmental crackdowns on carwash owners, and subsequently the placing of "No Engine Washing" signs at many coin-op carwashes.

The third option is to take your car to a place that does engine steam-cleaning. Before the general availability of good consumer engine cleaners in spray cans, this was the only option, and you had to "know where to go" to even find a carwash that did engine steam-cleaning. As the name implies, the process involves a pressure spray of really hot water and solvent. It really does a superb job of cleaning baked-on grease and dirt from engines, transmissions, and chassis. Many professional restorers make the steam-cleaner their first stop after buying a new project car. They have everything steam-cleaned even before they trailer their latest find home. That way they have a nice, clean base to work from for disassembly and restoration. The only drawback to steam-cleaning is that it may take any loose paint off along with the grease, but to the restorer or person

9.11 After the greasy areas have begun dissolving from the chemicals, the steam-cleaning unit is brought out. Experienced detailers know where to aim the spray to avoid wetting down your ignition, and are familiar with drying-out techniques for most popular vehicles.

9.12 Even the underside of the hood is steam-cleaned. For a few dollars more, you can probably have the detail shop also clean your front suspension, radiator or some other area for you.

who is going to go all the way with engine compartment detailing, it doesn't matter because they plan to repaint most components anyway. Check your Yellow Pages to find a shop that still offers steam-cleaning. Unfortunately, environmental restrictions have drastically affected that business as well, and many shops have quit steam-cleaning rather than install special underground sludge traps and filters. Steam-cleaning, if you can find a shop to do it, cleans everything extensively, but the main drawback is that it can remove paint from the engine or accessories if that paint isn't in perfect shape. Another problem is with moisture, which usually doesn't mix well with ignition and carburetion components. The steamy, pressurized water can get inside your distributor cap and other places that you think are completely sealed. Chances are that your engine won't start after a good steam bath.

Keeping the critical components dry during engine cleaning is a precaution that should be taken no matter what wash method you use - hose, pressure-wash or steam. If you are doing your washing at home or at the coin-op carwash (wherever you have access to electricity), remember to bring an electric hair dryer, which can be helpful to dry out ignition components or carpeting and upholstery that you have shampooed. The best idea is to avoid getting water on sensitive components in the first place. On computer-managed engines, the main computer "black box" is usually located under the dash area and is quite safe from engine washing, but on some vehicles the computer is tucked into the chassis, so find out where yours is before spraying.

9.13 For a more involved driveway cleanup than with the Toyota, we used this Ranger pick-up with 160,000 hard miles and lots of dusty, desert usage.

9.14 We used Castrol Super-Clean for the bulk of the engine cleaning, and found it to work great. It doesn't leave a film of its own on parts you decide to repaint, and, as long as it is rinsed off thoroughly, doesn't harm aluminum components. You'll find it handy enough for projects that the gallon jug and refillable dispenser are a good choice.

9.15 For hitting tight spots low on the engine, there's no beating a spray can like this Gunk degreaser, which puts out a veritable pinpoint spray stream.

Other than the brain box, the items to be protected include the coil, distributor, and carburetor. These can be effectively covered with household aluminum foil, plastic baggies, or "stretch-type" plastic food wrap. It's best to remove the air cleaner housing, both to make the cleaning easier around the intake manifold and also to more effectively wrap the carburetor. In years past, the advice was to somehow protect the spark plugs, too, but today's cars not only have higher-powered ignitions that start better, they also have plugs so buried that water would have a hard time grounding them out. If spark plug boots do get wet, take them off one at a time, dry with a tissue, then spray with a water-displacing lubricant like WD-40 or LPS. That should be enough to get you started. Sometimes the plastic or aluminum foil protection isn't enough to completely keep all moisture from the distributor cap, so if there's still a no-start, take off the distributor cap, wipe dry with tissues or hairdryer and put the cap back on.

After bagging or otherwise protecting vital components, use a pointed wooded stick, paint stirrer or even an old plastic-coated kitchen spatula to scrape away the heavier concentrations of grease. Look in crevices and places where dirt collects easiest. The more buildup you can remove this way, the fewer applications of cleaner you'll have to make. Don't use screwdrivers or other sharp metal tools or putty knives to remove the grease, or you take a chance on scrap-

9.16 Greasy areas will take second or third applications of spray degreaser, and you should use a parts-wash brush or old paintbrush to work it in and loosen stubborn deposits. The fluid level in this master cylinder was obscured by grime.

9.17 Your garden hose with a spray nozzle won't have the power of a steam-cleaner, but directed properly it will do the job. make sure painted or aluminum components are particularly-well rinsed.

ing up painted surfaces on the engine or components. If you scrape engine paint off, you'll have to repaint that area or the whole engine, both for appearance and to keep rust from developing on the bare metal.

In most cases it is not a good idea to do engine detailing on a hot engine. That had been the advice in years past, because heat does make the chemicals work faster in loosening dirt, but there are normally-hot components like the exhaust system (and turbocharger if you have one) that can crack if exposed to a sudden bath of cold water when the part is really hot. If you're doing your cleanup at the coin-op carwash, let the engine cool off while you are doing your interior vacuuming before starting the underhood detailing.

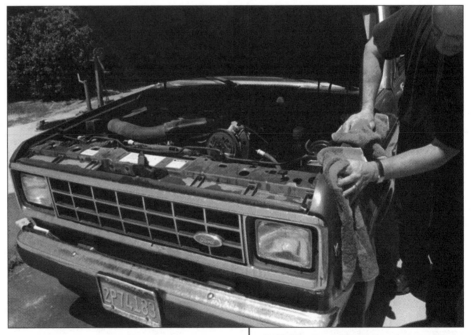

9.18 You could have used some kind of fender protection before starting your engine-cleaning project, but if you didn't, just make sure you towel off any water overspray from the exterior of the body. Droplets of chemical cleaner left to dry on your paint could cause streaking of your wax or even paint.

Begin your underhood cleanup by liberally applying your cleaner, even on areas that you don't think are that dirty. Douse the firewall, inner fender panels, radiator and all around the engine. Get down to the part of the chassis that is exposed in the engine compartment, too. Most engine cleaning products work best if they are not allowed to dry out completely before rinsing. If you notice that warmer areas seem to be drying out, spray them again with cleaner and let it work as long as the directions indicate it takes for thorough soaking of the deposits. Use a "parts cleaning" brush with a long wooden handle and stiff bristles to scrub the cleaner into areas of baked-on grease.

When your engine is covered with dirty, foamy film and you think it looks worse than when you started, start rinsing and a clean engine compartment will be magically revealed. It's important that your rinsing be very thorough. Many of the engine cleaners will soften paint and discolor chrome or aluminum components if not rinsed off completely with clean water. It's the rinsing phase where the use of a pressure-washer or the wand at the coin-op carwash are very helpful. They have the power to really blow dirt away, as well as having a wand that makes it easier to get into small areas than when using a garden hose. Please use some sort of eye protection when hosing off the engine cleaner. They can be very harmful to your eyes, and a pair of plastic safety goggles is inexpensive insurance.

By hand, wash the air cleaner housing you removed earlier, dry it and, if the paint is in good shape, give it a shot of cleaner/wax to bring the shine back. If the paint is scratched or still looks dull even after cleaner/wax, it should be repainted. This is the minimum for engine detailing because the air cleaner housing is large, easily detailed and is the most visible component when the hood is opened.

You will notice that some areas of the engine compartment are still dirty and require a second shot of cleaner, then a final rinse. Small areas of dirt can be treated with cleaner, rags, small brushes, and even cotton swabs, then rinsed with a spray bottle of clean water. After the rinsing, dry off large areas with rags, and use absorbent paper towels to dry up smaller areas. Do not use either a wash mitt or cotton toweling unless you can dedicate them to dirty jobs only. Don't wash out a sheepskin mitt used underhood and expect to use it another time on your paint job.

Since you are probably using strong cleaners on your underhood session, make sure that you either mask off your fenders and cowl, or wash down those areas with carwash soap and water right after the engine work. The cleaner and sludge you hose off can get on your paint and cause wax streaking, if not paint damage, when left on too long.

It's best to do as complete a job as possible during this session of engine cleaning so that you don't have to do such extensive cleaning again for a long time. After you have detailed and repainted a lot of the accessories, you don't want to get cleaner and waterspots on them unless absolutely necessary.

Hoses and small details

After a thorough cleaning, it's now a good time to examine all your engine compartment hoses, wires, belts and vacuum lines. If some of your hoses are noticeably spongy or soft, it's time to replace them. If all your rubber parts are in good shape, they can be made to look like new very easily. Clean them with a rag and any tire or rubber cleaner; then wipe with protectant. You'll be amazed at how fresh they look now, with minimal effort. Do not use cleaners or protectants on belts; this can cause them to slip and squeal. Spark plug wires that have become greasy from handling during plug changes are also easily cleaned and renewed. A used distributor cap that is still serviceable on the inside can look new again on the outside with a little touch of protectant.

9.19 Compare this photo of the Ranger's master-cylinder area to its "before" state. Here the fluid level is easy to see; everything looks clean, the hoses have been treated with protectant and the brake booster looks shiny again. Small areas or subsystems of your engine compartment can be done like this a little at a time.

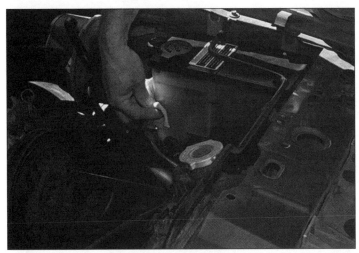

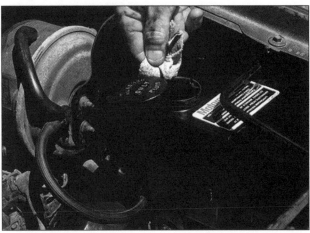

9.20 The fluid level in this windshield washer/overflow tank is now visible again, and the plastic is renewed with nothing more than a wipe-down with vinyl protectant.

9.21 Cleaning thoroughly around the filler cap means that the next time you open it to add washer fluid your hands will remain clean, which is how engine detailing can improve maintenance by making it less of a messy chore.

9.22 This power-steering fluid dipstick is not a pleasure to check. Small parts like this that are easily removable are best detailed off the car.

9.23 Several soakings with spray degreaser and some action with an old paintbrush got most of the grime off. What was left was cleaned with paper towels and cotton swabs.

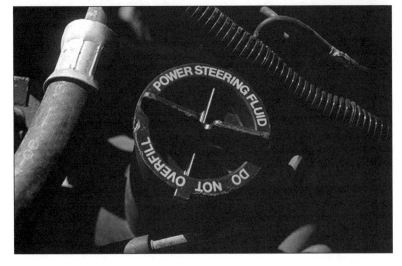

9.24 Back on the power steering pump, the dipstick is clean, easy to read and will probably be checked more frequently from now on.

9.25 Many engine compartment components are plastic today, which means that they don't rust and a few minutes with cleaner and protectant finds them as good as new. Here an AC hose has been removed from a clip to better detail the fan shroud. Put hoses and wires back into their clips when you're done for a factory appearance.

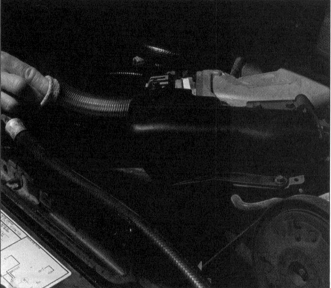

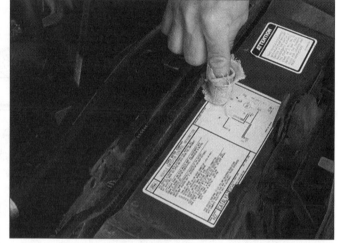

9.27 Do not use any harsh cleaners on your important emissions decals in the engine compartment or the writing could fade. Just use soap and water on a sponge or rag.

9.26 Check your hoses for cracks or sponginess. If they're OK, then some cleaner and protectant will bring them dramatically back to life.

9.28 This vacuum canister for the cruise control is a good example of a subsystem that won't be improved by minor detailing. It is rusty and needs to be removed, sanded, primed and painted. With 45 minutes' work, it can be back on looking as good as new.

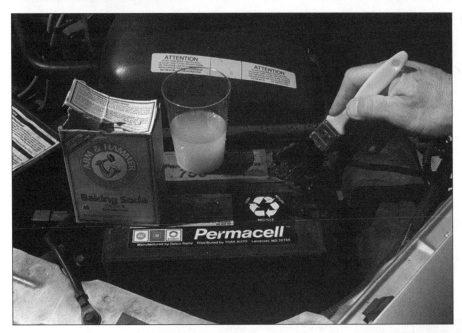

9.29 One area of the engine compartment that must be kept spotless is the battery. The terminals and battery top can be easily cleaned with some baking soda in water. We used a little cup of solution and an old paintbrush. This neutralizes corrosion and then is rinsed off with water.

9.30 After a cleaning, the top of the battery case can be renewed with a rag and a little vinyl protectant.

The top of your battery is probably the second-most visible accessory item under the hood, so clean it thoroughly. Clean the terminals and cable ends with baking soda and water to neutralize any corrosion, clean the contact areas, and reassemble with silicone spray or hand-applied grease to cover the cable ends to slow the inevitable reappearance of that green and white gook that can grow on an untended battery. This pays mechanical benefits, by keeping the starting and charging systems supplied with full voltage, and appearance benefits. A clean battery top indicates a car-owner who cares. After cleaning (be sure you don't get any of the baking soda/water mix into the filling holes of the battery as it could neutralize the necessary acid in the cells), the top of the battery case can be shined with a dose of protectant. While you're at it, check the battery for loose, rusted or missing battery hold-downs. New ones are inexpensive at the auto parts store, and they help "detail" the top of the battery as well as secure the battery in place.

The underside of your hood itself can probably use the same cleaning treatment as the engine. It should probably be cleaned first so that you aren't hosing off dirt onto an already-cleaned engine. If your hood is body-color painted on the engine side, just use carwash soap on it, using a soft brush to scrub dirt out of crevices near the inner stiffening ribs; then rinse and dry with lots of paper towels. A good car cleaner/wax should be all the polishing and protection you'll need after that. Many hoods have insulation on the engine side, and this can really accumulate engine oil vapors and road dirt. If it is fiberglass insulation, there isn't too much you can do to detail it, short of replacement with a new insulating mat (and total detailing would almost require that, considering how large an area is covered by the mat and how visible it is) but the newer plastic covered mats can be cleaned with most rubber or vinyl cleaners and given minor gloss with protectant. You don't want the mats to be shiny, so make sure you really buff off the excess protectant. Some brands of protectant or dressing are less glossy than others and would be appropriate for underhood mats.

9.31 It's helpful to set up a simple "clothesline" outside for the spray-painting of small engine or chassis components you remove. Use coathanger wire to suspend them so you can spray all sides of the item.

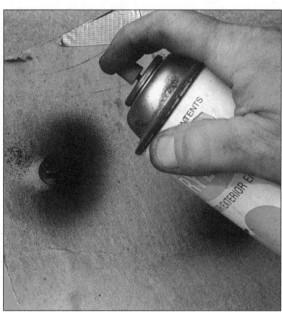

9.32 Even fasteners can be renewed with cleaning and some semi-flat black spray paint. Use a piece of cardboard with pencil holes punched into it to hold the bolts conveniently for spraying just the heads.

9.33 Valve covers are a prominent upper-engine feature, and along with the air cleaner housing are the most commonly and easily painted engine parts. We will follow the process of detail painting with a neglected aluminum valve cover. You may have stamped steel covers that need cleaning, fine sanding and painting only.

9.34 The valve cover has been removed from the engine and the gaskets surfaces scraped clean. Now it is doused liberally with degreaser, which is worked in and out of the details with a scrub brush.

9.35 Put on another application of degreaser and let it sit according to the product's directions, in this case about five minutes. On aluminum parts, don't let the cleaner sit on the part too long; it can dull the finish.

9.36 A thorough rinsing is necessary to remove the grime and all traces of the chemical cleaner.

9.37 Before any painting, the old paint must be prepped. On a steel cover the original paint would be wet-sanded smooth with #320 or #400 paper. On the details in this finned cover, fine steel wool is used to remove any loose paint or remaining dirt.

9.38 This is where some of the elbow grease is required: polishing. We're using Mother's Mag & Aluminum Polish. Compare the already-polished right side to the untouched areas at left. The tops of all of the fins must be polished too.

9.39 With newspaper and masking tape, the areas not to be painted are masked off and the cover can be painted with engine-specific spray paint. Several light coats are better than one heavy coat.

9.40 When the paint is dry, at least an hour later, peel away the masking and begin wiping paint off the highlights with lacquer thinner and a rag wrapped around your fingertip.

9.41 A light touch with the rag and thinner is all that is needed. Be patient and go slowly. Using too much thinner on the rag will put wet thinner down into the painted valleys and dull the paint or even remove it. Get the worst of the paint off in the first pass; then let it dry a few minutes before lightly going over the remaining traces of paint on the fin tops.

9.42 The rewards speak for themselves when you compare the rejuvenated valve cover with the one yet to be cleaned. The accent color is the color of the rest of the engine and will look great in place.

9.43 Of course, the valve covers must be reinstalled on the engine with new gaskets and RTV sealant. It's a small detail, but we used blue silicone to match the blue of the Ford engine.

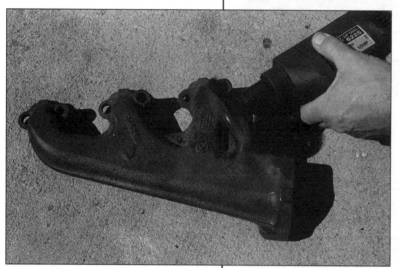

9.44 Once the air cleaner housing and valve covers have been detailed, the exhaust manifolds are usually the next to tackle because they usually are quite rusty. This tubular header is being removed for coating with high-temperature aluminum-chrome-look finish. Several sources for this kind of coating are listed in the Sourcelist at the end of this book.

9.45 The simplest treatment for standard cast-iron exhaust manifolds is to clean them thoroughly of rust, using chemical rust-removers, sandblasting or using a wire-brush attachment in your electric drill.

9.46 There are special paints available that give manifolds a "new cast-iron" look, yet protect the parts from rust, or you can use readily-available high-heat exhaust paint (sometimes also called barbecue paint). There are several colors of this paint, but most enthusiasts use flat black.

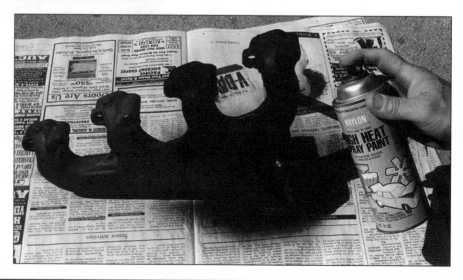

9.47 With the exhaust removed, this engine will be a lot easier to repaint and detail. Next the oil filter is removed, so that painting can be more thorough. The filter pad area itself will be masked off.

9.48 Household aluminum foil makes a great masking tool because it can be formed to go around most anything, like this steering joint. All of the engine surfaces that are going to be painted must be thoroughly cleaned before masking.

9.49 Here the valve cover area, firewall, steering, oil pan, water pump and other areas have been masked off, using foil, duct tape and newspaper with masking tape. Even the tops of the head studs have been masked, so their black color will contrast better with the engine color. The finished product will look less like it was hastily painted, and more like it had been rebuilt.

9.50 Several light coats of Ford blue engine paint are bringing this engine back to fresh-looking status with only an hour or two of prep work.

9.52 Spark plug wires can become grimy with time, but a little vinyl cleaner on a rag run over the length of the wires puts them right back into shape.

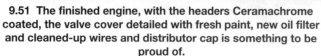

9.51 The finished engine, with the headers Ceramachrome coated, the valve cover detailed with fresh paint, new oil filter and cleaned-up wires and distributor cap is something to be proud of.

9.53 The top of the distributor cap and the spark plug boots can all be treated to a little protectant to make them look like new again.

9.54 This is in the realm of accessorizing, but most auto supply stores have special spark plug wire separators that dress up the wires and also prevent crossfiring.

9.55 New air cleaner and valve cover decals can be obtained from restoration sources and really put a finishing touch on repainted engine components.

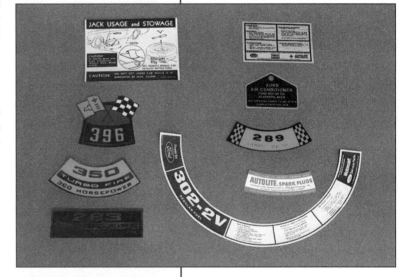

9.56 Only two kinds of enthusiast go to this much trouble to detail an engine compartment. The "motorhead" who has the bulk of the time and money of the whole car project right there under the hood or the "complete restoration" type owner who does the car from bumper to bumper and overlooks nothing. An underhood area like this is a pleasure to look at and work on.

Notes

10

Chassis

10 chassis

This section is for those readers interested in complete detailing of a vehicle. Even pro detailers would agree that very little attention to chassis detailing is worthwhile for a basic daily-driver or family car, beyond normal washing underneath to remove accumulated dirt. However, there are many enthusiasts who own collector cars, performance cars or other specialty vehicles who do spend extensive time detailing the underside of the vehicle to almost the same state of cleanliness as the outside of the body. Obviously, this requires considerable time to achieve what we have been calling our "detailing baseline," as well as quite regular inspections and follow-up cleaning. Those readers who have four-wheel-drive vehicles must maintain even more vigilance because the terrain they often travel on is dusty and muddy. Four-wheelers are often raised up high for extra

10.1 It may be hard for the average daily driver to imaging lavishing such attention on the undercarriage of a car, but specialty-car enthusiasts often have chassis and running gear as clean as the interior and as glossy as the paint work. Just basic cleaning underneath your car does have real advantages in making maintenance easier.

10.2 Four-wheel-drive vehicles, particularly those that have been raised extensively, have a dual problem. They spend lots of time in dirty conditions, and their whole chassis is much more exposed to view than a passenger car.

tire clearance (ostensibly, though many are raised just for that "off-road racer" look), and of course on these vehicles much more of the chassis is exposed to view, requiring extra consideration for chassis detailing **(see illustration).**

As with the engine detailing discussed in the previous chapter, there are also enthusiasts who like to add performance equipment to their chassis as well as to the engine and may do things to the chassis to improve appearances beyond just cleaning and painting. Adding chromed accessories, skid plates, extra shocks with bright-colored protective boots and other components are common modifications that often combine function with better looks **(see illustration).**

Your choices in chassis cleaning are roughly the same as with the engine compartment. You can get to your detailing baseline with professional steam-cleaning, pressure-washer, or just chemical spray cleaners and your garden hose. You'll find the same, stiff-bristled brush you used on your engine to be very helpful again in chassis and suspension cleaning. After the initial cleaning and rinsing phase, the rest of the detailing amounts to tedious cleaning of the small areas and perhaps repainting of some of the components. As we mentioned in the previous chapter, if you are maintaining a strictly-stock-factory look, then you should use whatever type of paint was used originally, in both color and gloss. Most chassis components are not painted a glossy color or a flat color, but with a semi-gloss or "chassis" black paint, which is available in spray cans or bulk. In your auto store, the major lines of spray paints include semi-gloss or "semi-flat black," and the companies that sell detailing products (see Sourcelist at the end of the book) carry special chassis-black paint as well.

10.3 The visibility of 4WD suspension systems means that detailing underneath is more important than on standard vehicles, and many four-wheelers routinely add custom aftermarket suspension components which call out for even more detailing and cleaning attention than stock parts.

10.4 In the case of late-model Corvettes like this, where do your draw the line between engine detailing and chassis detailing? When opening the flip front-end, everything is exposed to view, so all that forged-aluminum suspension should be kept as pristine as the high-tech engine.

As with the engine compartment, one of the advantages of going for a de-tailed look is that you get to carefully examine a lot of areas and components you haven't looked at for some time. You can discover leaks, loose brackets and fasteners and other potential problems before they get serious.

As you clean and detail, look for looseness in shocks, wheel bearings, balljoints, tie rod ends, driveshaft U-joints, motor and transmission mounts, spring shackles, U-bolts, etc. Inspect the fuel tank for signs of leaks and follow the fuel line all the way down the chassis, from tank to engine, looking for any leaks. If you have a hard-to-get-at fuel filter mounted on your chassis where it is "out of sight, out of mind," now's the perfect time to re-place it with a new filter, especially if yours is a fuel-injected vehicle. Fuel-injected cars have higher fuel line pressure, so check your Haynes repair manual first before changing the filter to find the recommended procedure for your model. Other leaks to look for underneath include transmission fluid, and you should examine the transmission pan, dipstick where it enters the transmission or pan (an O-ring seal may be leaking here) and the cooling lines that go forward to the bottom of your radiator. Obviously, any leak in your transmission fluid can spell big repair bills if you don't catch it early, and after you have done your detail cleaning any future leaks will be much easier to spot.

Under-the-car detailing usually requires getting the vehicle up first, so you have room to examine and work on components. There are basically two ways to do this, either yourself or at a shop. The latter is the best method, on a professional hoist. This is eminently safer and you can get the undercarriage to whatever height you need to make a close examination and perform your detailing. If you know someone who has a shop hoist, see if they will let you use it in off hours. Many technical schools and colleges have shop facilities you may be able to rent time in, or if you are in the military there is usually a free autoshop facility on the base. You may just have to find a local shop and ask them if they will rent you hoist time. This can be difficult at times, because some shops are wary of having outsiders work there on their own cars and may tell you that their "insurance prohibits any owner-done work." If you are looking for a facility, look for a four-post, above-ground hoist (with two

10.5 If you like automotive shop tools, detailing supplies and hard-to-find paints and materials, you need this catalog from Eastwood Company (see Sourcelist). They have an extensive assortment of chassis detailing paints and restoration tools.

10.6 Establish a relationship with a local shop that will lend or rent you their hoist once in a while when they are slow. Undercar detailing and even simple mechanical inspection is much easier when everything is at a working height. Muffler-shop hoists like this offer the best chassis accessibility.

long ramps you drive on) such as is commonly used at muffler shops because the single-post, infloor hoist at many gas stations has four big arms underneath your car that restrict access to cleaning and inspecting some spots **(see illustration)**.

If you are doing the work at home in your garage or driveway, use common sense and reasonable safety precautions to avoid accidents. Never work under a car that is supported only by a jack, even if for only a moment. Use solid jackstands and/or steel ramps, and locate them on strong parts of the chassis, not sheetmetal. Even with jackstands, you won't get the chassis up high enough for easy detailing, but a rolling mechanics creeper does help a lot compared to crawling underneath on your back. Obviously, you are doing a dirty job here, and you should wear old clothes or coveralls, preferably long-sleeve. If you are cleaning rusty areas with a drill-mounted wire brush or even just scraping greasy spots with a putty knife, it's best to also wear some kind of goggles for eye protection. If there is any rust underneath, such as on your exhaust system, it's very easy for it to fall in your face when you're lying on your back under there. And if you care at all about your hair, it's a good idea to wear an old baseball cap (brim turned to the back) to keep from applying the wrong kind of "greasy kid stuff" to your head.

Speaking of the exhaust system, this is a good time to examine your system for rustout, cracks, broken or missing hangers and potential leaks. You may be due for a new muffler, catalytic converter or a pipe or two. Just because you don't hear any extra exhaust noise when you're driving with the stereo on doesn't mean there isn't a potential problem. Even a small exhaust leak can allow dangerous carbon monoxide fumes into the car, giving you headaches or making you drowsy.

The exhaust system is also one of those areas where some car owners like to add an extra touch in detailing. The simplest and most common addition is a chromed exhaust tip. They are available inexpensively at any auto parts outlet in a wide variety of styles, shapes and lengths to suit any application, and can make a small difference in the appearance of the vehicle from the rear, something that just adds a little extra either in a luxury or performance look. The appearance of the muffler and tailpipe can often be de-

10.7 Once you get your car up on the hoist, it's an easy matter to go around with spray cleaner and rags getting rid of road grime caused by oil vapors mixed with road dust. In an hour or less, you should have most of the dirty areas taken care of, and perhaps the next time the lift is available, you might repaint some components or apply some spray can undercoating.

10.8 When priming or painting any of your engine or chassis parts, indeed any spray-painting where a smooth finish is desired, try warming the spray can of paint in a jar or bucket of warm water (not hot). The slight warming of the paint contents makes them mix up easier when you shake the can, and the warmed can has a little higher pressure for a finer spray.

10.9 On many cars, the rear view of the car is broken up by a distractingly-bright, shiny muffler hanging down underneath. Less than 30 seconds with a spray can of flat black high-heat exhaust paint on the back of the muffler can make a remarkable difference in the look from behind.

10.10 Notice how clean the rear view is on this car, where the exhaust "blends in" better with the chassis by being dull black. There is no distraction from the body lines except the tailpipe tip.

tailed easily with a spraycan of flat black exhaust paint. On many cars, the rear of the muffler is exposed at the back of the car, hanging down underneath the rear bumper area. Mufflers are usually coated with bright plating that calls attention to the muffler when looking at the car from the rear. It's a small detail, but when you just spray the back of the muffler with some flat black, it can make the shiny muffler "disappear" into the rest of the undercarriage, allowing the rear of the car to look simpler, cleaner and focus more attention on the new tailpipe tip **(see illustration)**. Some of the newer luxury imports do this from the factory; they have flat-blacked mufflers and factory chrome or even-gold-rimmed exhaust tips, so the rear view is a just a little "tidier." The flat-black treatment may also be applied to the fuel tank if that item is bright-plated and hangs down into view from under the rear bumper. Blacking it out just seems to show off the styling of the car and bumper better by not creating a visual distraction.

10.11 Although this transmission is out of the car for photographic purposes, we'll illustrate how any rough cast-iron or cast-aluminum engine or chassis part can be cleaned to look like new.

Another spot where one chassis component can be a visual distraction is the shock absorbers. Aftermarket replacement shocks are usually painted some bright color like orange, red, white or blue for in-store sales appeal. If you want that look under your car, that's fine, but often you see a car several years old going down the road ahead of you, and the entire undercarriage is old and neutral looking, except that there are these neon-like shock absorbers hanging there. It's obvious that the car just came from a shock sale at the discount tire-and-brake shop. Those new shocks tend to visually leap out at you, and a few shots of flat-black spraypaint on them can tame the view down and eliminate the distraction.

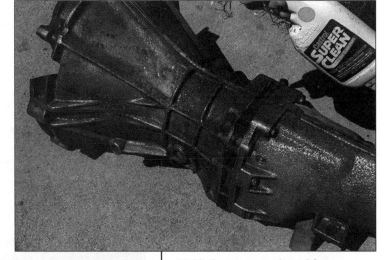

On high-riding four-wheel-drives, chassis and suspension appearance is more noticeable, and you may want to go beyond straight cleaning to touch up components that are rusty or whose paint is chipped. Watch your overspray, and use aluminum foil, masking tape and newspaper or kitchen "clingwrap" plastic to cover areas you don't want painted. You are working in a confined environment, with your face close to the work, so it is important to wear a breathing mask anytime you are doing repainting under the chassis. Chromed accessories should be cleaned and protected by cleaner/wax just like outside chrome, and rubber parts should be cleaned and

10.12 A strong coating of Super-Clean over all of the transmission, not just the dirty areas, will result in a uniform look when you're done.

10.13 A short, brass-bristled wire brush (in this case a barbecue grille brush) should be used to scrub the cleaner on the dirtiest areas to loosen grime. If any area dries out or the brush is bogging down, spray on more cleaner.

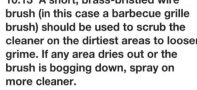

treated with protectant. You're accomplishing several things here. You are making the undercarriage look more like it did when it was new, the parts are going to be much better protected from dirt, moisture, road salts, etc. and if you ever do have to do any chassis work or maintenance it will be a much more pleasant job when you are working in a clean environment.

After you reach your baseline, regular washing and rinsing under the vehicle will keep this area looking good without great effort and is especially important if you live in an area of the country where there are serious winters. The sand and salt used on the roads in snow country will collect under your vehicle and are major contributors to chassis and underbody rusting. Many drivers in hard-winter areas never touch or look at the underside of their vehicle for the entire winter, but once you have gone to the trouble of doing undercar detailing you'll

10.14 Although it still looks grimy, the first blast of clean water from your hose nozzle will reveal a much cleaner surface. For some, this is detailed enough.

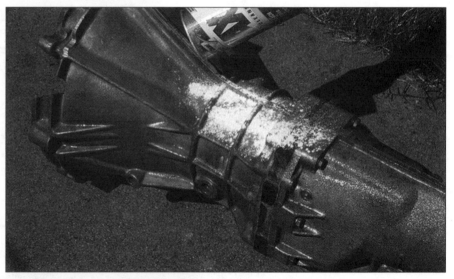

10.15 If you still have grimy areas where dirt is caked into rough areas in the casting, wet it down with water and sprinkle on some powdered household cleanser.

10.16 Working the wet cleanser like a loose paste, scrub with a brass wire brush and the end result will be cast aluminum that looks like it just came off the assembly line.

have a better picture of overall car preservation, and you'll be more inclined to do a thorough wash and rinse underneath, at least a few times during the long winter. Hot or even warm water is best for such cleaning in winter, so you probably want to have this done at a carwash or use the coin-op carwash.

Most chassis components that you wind up having to paint because of rust should be painted in two steps: primer and finish coat. A number of suitable primers are available in spray cans, in both light and dark colors. Generally, you should use a color of primer that best matches the finish color you intend to apply - light primer under light colors, dark primer under black. This reduces the number of coats of top color required to completely and evenly cover the primer. Let the primer dry according to the directions on the can, then apply finish coats. As with most spray paints, two light coats are better than one heavy one, with more even coverage and less chance of runs. If you are going for a glossy finish on the part, you should use a "sandable" primer, and dry or wet-sand it with 320-grit sandpaper, then clean with a tack-rag before finish painting. This will take out any little "nits" in the primer coat and make the finish coat glossier. For parts that you are just trying to protect, there are anti-rust primers that can be applied in several coats without the need for a different topcoat.

Rust, depending on the region you drive in, may be a large problem in trying to maintain the resale value of your vehicle. In areas with harsh winters, many cars rust out long before their mechanical parts give out, due to the salts used to melt ice from the roads. It's like giving the underside of your car a salt-water bath, only worse, because snow and ice may stay packed and concentrated under your chassis and fenderwells long after it's gone from the roads, giving the water and salt longer to work on your metals. A large business is done every year in the Midwest and East in aftermarket undercoating or rust prevention. The new-car dealers there also commonly offer extra undercoating protection as an extra-cost option when you buy a car. These aftermarket shops and dealers may or may not do a thorough job of undercoating, some do only the easy-access areas.

You can do a lot for the longevity of your vehicle by doing a little preventative undercoating yourself with very little investment. Large spray cans of undercoating are available in auto parts stores that can be sprayed by the do-it-yourselfer **(see illustration)**. These paints are thick materials with tars in them for long-lasting protection. With some time spent masking, and using the kind of spray nozzle with a little tube in it, you can be quite accurate in application,

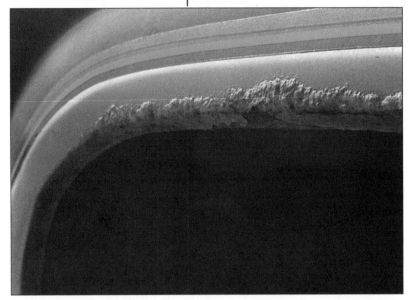

10.17 Rust is a serious problem in any state where road salts are used, and this fenderwell lip is merely the exterior "tip of the iceberg" as far as chassis corrosion goes. This kind of damage can be slowed or eliminated by periodic chassis cleaning (even during winter) and the use of undercoaters and rustproofers.

10.18 Use a rubberized undercoater on your cleaned and dried fenderwells. On vehicles that have plastic inner fender panels, try to get the spray up behind them.

10.19 Most rustproofing kits include the spray can, nozzles for spraying in hidden areas and new rubber plugs to fill any holes you may have had to drill for access.

without unwanted overspray on driveline parts or the exhaust system. Obviously, such rust-beaters should be applied only after a thorough cleaning, and you must be careful to mask off the outside of the body, particularly the rocker panels, to prevent overspray onto the body paint. Most of the undercoaters describe themselves as being "rubberized", which means that they are not only flexible, but have the secondary benefit of minor sound deadening as well. They are particularly helpful in fenderwells, and on cars that don't have inner splash shields. They can reduce the possibility of "starchips" caused by the tires flinging gravel up from underneath and causing chips in the exterior paint on the fenders. Most cars do have inner fenderwells to prevent this (and to prevent snow from building up in inaccessible areas, causing rustout), and in fact, because of the rust problems, many newer vehicles have plastic inner fender panels. Those plastic inner panels can be cleaned with water pressure at the carwash, then treated with vinyl protectant to make them easier to clean later on.

Rubberized undercoatings do not do a total job of preventing rust, but they help, and there are several specialized coatings available in spray cans that are specifically for rust prevention **(see illustration)**. Usually, these sprays contain some kind of water repellent like soluble wax or silicones. Kits are available that contain an extended spray nozzle to get into small areas. These rustproofers work best on areas not accessible to regular undercoating sprays, but you have to somehow get access to those panels to treat them. This may involve drilling some small holes in rocker panels, door bottoms and inner fender panels. Some rustproofing kits include rubber plugs to reseal any holes you have to drill to spray through with the nozzle.

Sometimes car doors already have drain holes in the bottom, and these

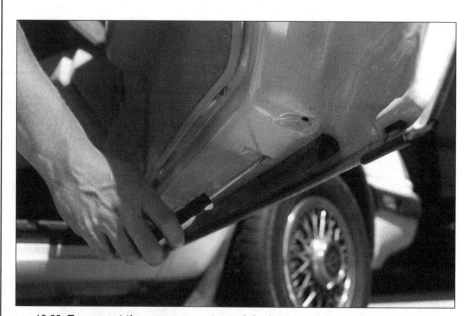

10.20 To prevent the common rustout of the bottom of doors, first locate any factory drain holes in the inner bottom edge of the door. If they are clogged, water will collect in the door and start corrosion. Clear the drainholes with a screwdriver or wire.

10.21 Using one of the long nozzles in the rustproofing kit, spray inside of the door bottom, angling the spray to get all possible coverage inside.

10.22 Inside the fenderwell is another critical area. Clean the area thoroughly and dry it out, with a hairdryer if necessary.

should be cleaned out with a length of coathanger wire or a screwdriver **(see illustration)**. Water runs down your windows normally, and if the door-bottom holes are clogged with leaves or dirt, water will collect there and cause rust. With the windows rolled up to keep the waxy spray off the glass, insert the rustproofer nozzle through the holes and spray, trying to get a coating on the inside of the door bottom **(see illustration)**. Another area to spray with rustproofer is the inside lip of the fenderwells **(see illustration)**. This is best done with the car on jackstands and the wheels removed. Use a stiff brush to clean any collected dirt from the inner fender lips, but be careful when running your hand around the inside to check. The inner edges of the fender can be sharp, especially if you have chromed trim around the lip. Rocker panels can be easily rustproofed by removing the door sillplate trim and drilling into an area covered by those trim pieces **(see illustration)**. You can do a thorough job when spraying in from the top, in-

10.24 If you were using factory holes to spray rustproofer through, replace the stock rubber plugs, or use the kit plugs if you had to drill new holes.

10.23 Rocker panels are very close to the road, have hidden areas and are one of the first areas to rust out. Remove the door sillplates to expose the top of the rocker panels. Either use factory holes as shown or drill a few holes to insert the rustproofer spray nozzle to get full coverage inside the rockers.

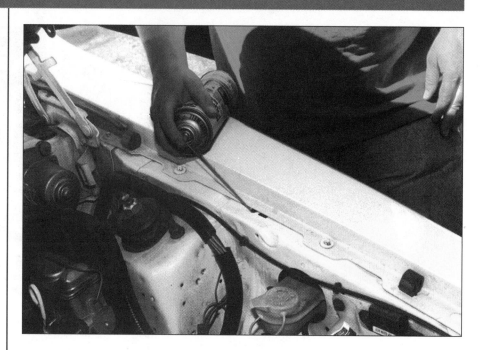

10.25 Start your rustproofing by spraying areas where holes do not have to be drilled, such as where the fender bolts to the inner fender panel in the engine compartment. The idea is to get the spray to the hidden part of the fender.

stead of up from underneath. To get at rear fenderwells, you may have to remove some kickpanels or upholstery panels to get rustproofing in there. If the trim-retainer holes are big enough, you may be able to spray without drilling any new holes.

All of this attention to parts of the car you normally never see may seem superfluous, but if you are dealing with a car you just bought and whose history you don't know, or you just plan for your car to last you for many years to come, under-the-car detailing and rust prevention will pay off in the long run.

11

Tires/wheels

11 Tires/wheels

Second to the color and gloss of your vehicle's paintwork, there is perhaps no other visual aspect of detailing more important than your tires and wheels. Car enthusiasts agree almost universally that paint and wheel/tire choice are the two biggest factors in a car's visual appeal. Even a car with ugly styling can make a great impression with the right paint and the right wheels **(see illustration)**. This is a totally subjective judgement - not everyone agrees on what the best color or wheel choice is for any particular vehicle, but all agree that wheels and tires are key to establishing a desired "look." For such enthusiasts, and those readers with factory wheels and "ordinary" tires, this chapter has an abundance of solid information on detailing them for beauty and protection - you don't need to have a hot rod to feel good about putting effort into tire and wheel detailing.

11.1 Nice wheels and tires are second only to a good paint job in a car's overall appearance. Even a car with somewhat dowdy styling can be really stunning with a great paint job and the right tires and wheels.

Basic washing

The first step in tire/wheel detailing is actually part of your basic vehicle washing. You have to be very careful about what kind of cleaners are used on your wheels, depending on their material and surface finish, but the carwash soaps we have recommended for body washing are mild enough to use on your wheels and tires, too. Beyond soap and water, there are very few cleaners that can work equally well on wheels and tires, and on wheels they are particularly specialized. Because your tires are probably dirtier than the body, and your front wheels may have brake dust particles coating them, it's advisable to use a separate wash mitt, terrycloth or sponge for your wheels and tires. Do not use this mitt for anything but tires and wheels; otherwise the dirt from your wheels/tires could be damaging to your paint if embedded in the mitt, particularly with the residue from metallic brake pads. While you are washing, soap up and rinse off the fenderwells and inner fender lips first, to avoid dripping water and dirt onto clean wheels and tires.

A plastic-bristled household brush is very helpful in the initial stages of cleaning, to work the soap into tire and wheel crevices, dislodging accumulated dirt. Small areas around valve stems, wheel weights and lug nut recesses may require a small, artist's brush to clean. As we have cautioned in other areas of detailing, the wheels and tires should be cold when you wash them, because heat can make chemical cleaners work unevenly or too aggressively. Use plenty of sudsy soap when scrubbing tires and wheels, and don't let the solution dry out on the tire before you are ready to rinse. The dirt must be kept in suspension and lubricated with soap to rinse off easily. The pros don't waste water when cleaning, but they do know that there's "no such thing as too much rinsing," especially when specialty aluminum wheels are involved. It may seem like a small point, but your wheel brushes and wash mitt should also be rinsed thoroughly with clean water before being put away.

After the basic wash and rinse, the rest of your tire/wheel detailing procedures will depend on the type of wheels you have.

Painted wheels and hubcaps

If you have full-coverage factory wheel covers, getting to a detailing baseline may require removing all four wheel covers before the wash phase. This way the steel wheel can be thoroughly cleaned of dirt and brake dust. This also allows you to thoroughly scrub the backside of the wheel covers, which are probably equally coated with dust (see illustrations). If you don't remove the wheel covers, that brake dust is always there, ready to drip out onto a freshly detailed tire. If the cover is cleaned inside and out, at least the next time you drive through a puddle a potentially harmful mix of water and brake dust isn't going to run out in streaks.

The painted steel wheels your covers go on can be cleaned with most cleaner/waxes, which will give the paint some protection and make hosing off dirt on later cleanups that much easier. If there are chips in the paint, they can be detailed with a paper match dipped in touchup paint. You're not trying for a concourse look here, because the wheel is hidden behind the wheel cover, but you do want to address any spots where rust can develop. Steel wheels are often chipped around the outer edge where the gripping clips of the wheel cover grab onto the wheel. You may even decide that the entire wheel needs repainting for the best looks and prevention of future rust. The wheels should be removed for full painting, so that you can get to the usually-worn-bare areas around the lug nuts.

11.2 Even basic wheel covers need detailing. Once a year, you should carefully remove your full-circle wheel covers and check the backsides for brake dust.

11.3 Ordinary soap and water with a good stiff brush will loosen all of this metallic brake dust. Do front and rear and then rinse off, protecting the front side with plastic polish (ABS covers).

11.4 Brake drums should be periodically cleaned of rust with a drill fitted with a wire brush attachment, then sprayed with high-heat paint to slow further rusting. On wheels that expose part of the brake drum through the spoke holes, this little touch cleans up the overall appearance.

Clean and detail your tires before painting the wheels, since any overspray that gets past your masking and onto the tire will be much easier to remove from the rubber after it has been treated with dressing or protectant. Masking the wheel with the tire still on can be tedious because you have to curve the tape around the rim. Instead of using masking tape, you may want to make a thin masking tool out of cardboard. Curve it to the circumference of about a quarter of your wheel, tuck it into the groove where the tire meets the wheel, and keep moving it around the wheel as you paint new sections. Good automotive primer should be used after the wheel is sanded smooth, feathering out chips and cleaning rusted areas to bare metal. After two or three coats of primer, the wheel can be topcoated. If your wheels were painted body-color, you can find touch-up spray cans at the auto parts store that match that original paint for your make

11.5 Painted steel wheels with beauty rings and small hubcaps can be restored by careful sanding, priming and painting of the wheel, followed by polish and paste wax. Polish the trim rings and hubcaps while off the wheels, then reinstall carefully.

11.6 On bigger trucks and motorhomes, aftermarket wheels are very expensive due to the size involved, but the aftermarket offers full metal covers, either chromed steel or stainless steel, that look exactly like custom wheels. The covers can be polished with chrome cleaner or metal polish.

11.7 Typical of today's factory wheel that mixes a variety of surfaces and treatments, this Camaro aluminum wheel has a polished rim, an as-cast center, and a machined center cap. The as-cast center is clearcoated. Use only the wheel cleaner suited to the most fragile surface, the clearcoat, although the outer rim can be polished with mag cleaner.

11.8 Some aftermarket wheels have machined finish areas that must be treated carefully in order not to lose their character from too much polishing. Others, like this wheel, have a clear-coat to protect the fine groove lines in the machined area.

and year of vehicle.

If you have the wheels off for either cleaning or painting, now is a good time to check over your brake rotors, calipers and/or drums. Because of the constant heating and cooling cycles they go through, brake parts are subject to perennial rust. Brake drums can be cleaned with a wire brush to remove most of the rust (be sure to wear a dust mask), and painted with a high-heat exhaust paint in either black or dull silver **(see illustration)**. This will help slow future rust and also detail the drum, which can be seen through the holes or slots in many wheel designs. A polished wheel's good looks can be diminished when you see it bolted onto a rusty hub or drum.

Brake rotors should not be painted or wire-brushed in the wide, shiny area that the pads contact but often can be detailed by masking that area and just painting around the center/hub area and the outside edge beyond the pad-wear area. If you wire-brush and paint your calipers, be sure that you don't get paint onto the pads themselves or it could reduce their frictional abilities, and mask off the bleeder screws and brake hoses as well.

Repainting is much more important on those wheels that use a small hubcap because more of the painted wheel is exposed. You might consider taking a little extra time in repainting such wheels by wet-sanding the primer coats before applying the final color coats. This will make a smother finish. Some restorers take extra time painting steel wheels and even polish and wax the paint afterwards for a finish as colorful and glossy as the rest of the car.

With small-cap wheels and wheels with chromed or stainless trim rings, you must be careful when removing the hubcaps or rings not to damage either the wheel paint or the thin metal of these accessories because chips on these wheels will probably show. Don't use a sharp screwdriver as a pry tool unless absolutely necessary. Use your fingers if possible, or use a screwdriver whose

11.9 Right after your basic driveway wash, you may notice that your rear specialty wheels look great, but the fronts don't. The difference is the front wheels are coated with stubborn brake dust. If you rotate your tires regularly, all four wheels will need deep cleaning.

11.10 This tire and aluminum wheel need a thorough cleaning to achieve our detailing baseline.

edges have been smoothed off with a file and the tip coated with plastic. Hardware stores carry a plastic goop designed just for dipping the handles of tools, only this time you apply it to the tip to make a scratchless screwdriver. A hardwood dowel with the end flattened somewhat will remove all but the most stubborn hubcaps with less chance of scratching wheels than a steel pry tool.

Your stock hubcaps or full wheelcovers can be cleaned with detailing products appropriate for the material and finish. Plastic hubcaps should only be cleaned with plastic cleaner. Often, today's wheel covers feature delicate chromed plastic, with only plastic polish advisable. Many metal hubcaps are chromed or stainless steel, with basic chrome cleaner fine for the plated ones, and any metal polish suitable for the stainless, with a final coat of body wax recommended for protecting either type. If there are painted details within the design of the plastic or metal wheel cover, these can be made to look like new by repainting, but there is considerable labor involved in the tedious masking process.

When reinstalling hubcaps, trim rings or full wheel covers, take care not to damage them. Carefully align the valve stem hole to make sure you don't cut a stem (which also ensures the cap is going back on in the same orientation as it had been, not cutting any new scrapes in the wheel's paint), and do not use a rubber mallet. Yes, this has been the standard hubcap installing tool for decades, but many are too heavy for today's plastic wheel cover, causing dents, and even on metal trim rings and hubcaps the typical black-rubber hammer can leave black marks on the chrome. If a black hammer is all you have, put a piece of cardboard between the hubcap and the rubber hammer when driving caps back on, or use a soft plastic hammer. The bottom of your fist makes perhaps the best tool for the job. You can put a lot of force behind it, but it can't damage the wheel or the hubcap.

Cleaning specialty wheels

Most detailers have a basic procedure or order they follow when detailing a car. They don't all do it the same, but they all get beautiful results. One area where there is some disagreement is in the tire and wheel cleaning. Which do you do first? The bottom line is that it doesn't matter as long as you develop your

11.11 Start with just a more thorough washing with soap and water, using a short-bristled brush to scrub oxidized dead rubber from the tires, especially around the lettering. Don't use the brush on the wheels.

11.12 Rinse the wheel and tire well, with good pressure from your hose nozzle.

own routine and it works for you. Some detailers do the tires first, others, do the wheels first. What's important in either case is not getting the cleaners, protectants or waxes from one surface onto the other.

Our suggestion is to clean the wheels first, if only because there are easier ways to keep tire cleaners and dressing from getting on wheels than vice-versa. The pros recommend to do one wheel at a time, not to get all four wheels to the same state of cleaning at the same time, then run around to rinse them all off in sequence. The chemical cleaners shouldn't be on your wheels any longer than the instructions indicate and should not be allowed to dry out on the wheel before being rinsed off **(see illustrations)**.

The type of product you use to clean your wheels depends entirely on the

11.13a We're using Eagle One Aluminum Wash, sprayed over the whole wheel and allowed to set according to the directions.

11.13b Use a small section of sponge to work the cleaner in around wheel details and loosen grime.

11.14 Do only one wheel at a time so that wheel cleaner does not dry out or stay on the aluminum longer than recommended. Hose off thoroughly.

material and surface finish of the wheels - what is good for bare aluminum isn't good for chromed wire wheels (see Eagle One wheel chart). Despite the wide variety of wheels on the market today, there is a selection of wheel cleaners almost as big, and many of them claim to be suitable for all types of wheels. Most of the detailers we have talked with discount the universality of any wheel cleaner. In order to be safe for the most delicate finishes, it has to be made relatively weak, in which case it may not do the job on neglected wheels. The experts recommend getting exactly the right product for your application and then sticking with it.

First determine what type of wheels you have. If they are factory aluminum wheels, find out from your dealer exactly what the finish and cleaning recommendations are. If your wheels are truly factory-installed, and not dealer-installed, your owner's manual should tell you the proper cleaning procedures. If yours are aftermarket specialty wheels, consult the wheel manufacturer or a local custom wheel shop to determine the surface finish. The possibilities in aluminum wheels are: uncoated cast aluminum wheels, cast aluminum wheels with a machined or polished outer edge, fully-polished aluminum, chromed aluminum, chromed steel wheels, chromed steel wheels with painted and/or clearcoated centers, aluminum wheels with machined edge and painted or clearcoated areas, anodized aluminum and wire wheels which can be true wire wheels or "wire baskets" which have a removable, unitized wire set over a chromed steel wheel. Confusing, isn't it?

Because there are so many surface materials and finishes, find out what you have and use only the least aggressive product that it takes to get results. When there is a mixture of finishes on the same wheel, such as an aluminum wheel with a machined and clearcoated center but a polished rim, use only the cleaning product recommended for the most fragile of the finishes, in this case the clearcoated center. The newer clearcoated aluminum wheels, found on factory and aftermarket aluminum wheels, need the same cautions with abrasives as the clear-coat finish of your paint job. No one "all-purpose" wheel cleaner is going to be right, and the better known detailing product companies have a full range of wheel cleaners, with a dedicated product for each of the wheel finishes you will encounter. While you may have to buy only one or two wheel cleaning products, imagine the pro detailer who must have all of these products to handle whatever

11.15 The wheel is now 90% restored. Dry the wheel and tire with towels before going any further. If this wheel had been maintained more regularly, this would be all that is necessary for good wheel appearance in a regular cleanup.

he's called upon to detail.

The chrome-plated aluminum wheels we mentioned above are found only on expensive luxury and sports vehicles. Generally, these are cars that come factory equipped with distinctive aluminum wheels, not chromed. A few companies specialize in chrome-plating aluminum wheels (a difficult process not easily handled by standard plating shops) and offer the service to auto dealers. The aftermarket company buys sets of new Mercedes, Corvette or BMW wheels, has them plated and then offers them to dealers on an exchange basis. The "take-off" wheels they get from the dealers are then polished and plated and put in inventory. The process is expensive, but many luxury-car owners prefer the greater brilliance and easier wheel care of the chrome-plated versions. They can be detailed with mild chrome cleaners and waxed for protection.

11.16 This ugly brown "rash" around the polished part of the rim is the most stubborn part of the brake dust residue. It would never look this bad if regular wheel cleaning had been kept up.

11.17 Rags, elbow grease and mag polish are all that's required to bring the polished rim back to original beauty. Polish right up to the edge. Don't worry if a little polish gets on the tire; we're doing that next.

ALUMINUM/ANODIZED

RIM SECTION —
ANODIZED
ALUMINUM —

DESCRIPTION: Found primarily on aftermarket wheels manufactured in Japan—usually on outer rim section (Satin/semi-gloss lustre). Not as shiny as chrome or polished aluminum.

ROUTINE CLEANING:
Aluminum Wash
& Brightener

POLISHING/DETAILING:
5-Minute
Detailer

ALUMINUM/POLISHED

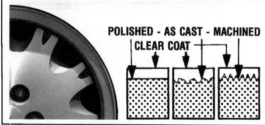

POLISHED SURFACE —
ALUMINUM —

DESCRIPTION: Very smooth surface, no visible grooves, high degree of shine. Polished outer rims are often combined with painted/clear-coated or "as cast" center sections. NOTE: If wheels of this type are extremely dirty and oxidized, use Mag Cleaner (UWC Symbol "B") for initial cleaning.

ROUTINE CLEANING:
All Finish
Wheel Cleaner

POLISHING/DETAILING:
5-Minute
Detailer

ALUMINUM/CLEAR COATED OR PAINTED

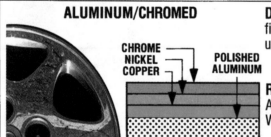

POLISHED - AS CAST - MACHINED
CLEAR COAT —

DESCRIPTION: Found primarily on aluminum wheels. Clear or colored, smooth protective coating. May show "orange peel" in finish like paint. When clear coat is applied over machine finish, fine grooves may still be visible beneath smooth clear coat.

ROUTINE CLEANING:
All Finish
Wheel Cleaner

POLISHING/DETAILING:
5-Minute
Detailer

ALUMINUM/CHROMED

CHROME
NICKEL   POLISHED
COPPER —   ALUMINUM

DESCRIPTION: Highest degree of shine, with a smooth, mirror-like finish. NOTE: If wheels of this type are extremely dirty and oxidized, use Wire Hubcap Cleaner (UWC Symbol "D") for initial cleaning.

ROUTINE CLEANING:
All Finish
Wheel Cleaner

POLISHING/DETAILING:
Mag & Chrome
Polish

*Uniform Wheel Care Systems

The Uniform Wheel Care System® was developed by major wheel manufacturers and Eagle One to provide consumers with a simple A-B-C method of determining the proper cleaning product to easily, effectively, and safely maintain their custom style/specialty wheels and hub caps.

All wheels manufactured by participating wheel companies have a Uniform Wheel Care label on their outer rim. This label identifies the proper wheel care product to be used and illustrates the specific Uniform Wheel Care Symbol® that is on the recommended cleaning product.

ALUMINUM/MACHINE FINISHED & "AS CAST"

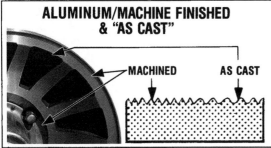

MACHINED   AS CAST

DESCRIPTION: Characteristic of most older mags—"Vector—Cyclone—Hurricane" finned style. Manufactured prior to 1980–81. Defined visible grooves (machine lines) often combined with rough, unfinished open pore, "as cast" sections.

ROUTINE CLEANING:
Mag Cleaner

POLISHING/DETAILING:
Mag & Chrome
Polish

STEEL/PAINTED OR CLEAR COATED

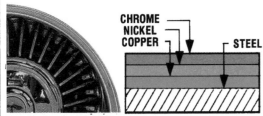

PAINT/CLEAR COAT
STEEL

DESCRIPTION: Clear or colored, protective coating, smooth with fine "orange peel."

ROUTINE CLEANING:
All Finish
Wheel Cleaner

POLISHING/DETAILING:
5-Minute
Detailer

STEEL/CHROMED

CHROME
NICKEL
COPPER   STEEL

DESCRIPTION: Highest degree of shine, with a smooth, mirror-like finish. NOTE: If heavily oxidized use Chrome Wire Wheel Kit (UWC Symbol "A") for initial cleaning.

ROUTINE CLEANING:
Wire & Chrome
Wheel Cleaner

POLISHING/DETAILING:
Mag & Chrome
Polish

WHEEL COVERS: Aluminum/Stainless Steel & ABS Plastic

DESCRIPTION: Any of a variety of wheel covers, dust caps or trim rings.

ROUTINE CLEANING:
Wire & Chrome
Wheel Cleaner

To find the proper wheel cleaning product for new or used wheels that do not have the label, Eagle One wheel care products have a Uniform Wheel Care recommendation chart on the package:

Ⓐ	Ⓑ	Ⓒ	Ⓓ	Ⓔ	Ⓕ
WIRE WHEEL CLEANING KIT	**MAG CLEANER**	**ALL FINISH** WHEEL CLEANER	**WIRE & CHROME** WHEEL CLEANER	**MAG & CHROME** POLISH	**ALUMINUM** WASH AND BRIGHTENER
For chrome plated wheels, wire wheels, wire baskets, chrome reverse, etc.	For machine finished (fine visible grooves), open pore "mag"/aluminum wheels.	For clear-coated, painted and/or polished aluminum and steel wheels.	For original equipment wire hubcaps (routine cleaning), and plastic mag style hubcaps.	For chrome plated steel & polished "mag"/aluminum wheels.	For anodized wheels, aluminum bumpers and running boards.

11.18 Eagle One has a full line of specialty wheel cleaners, each one designed for specific types of factory and aftermarket wheels. Most pro detailers suggest there is no such thing as a "universal" cleaner safe for all wheels.

While great care and the right product are required to handle clearcoated wheels, anodized and machine-finished wheels are also tricky. Like the clear paints, the anodizing (a special plating for aluminum, either clear or with a translucent color) can be ruined by using too aggressive a product. The anodized finish is great for protection, but it does not have the high shine and gloss of polished bare aluminum. Don't polish an anodized wheel expecting to get a mirror finish or you'll have cut through the protective anodizing. Likewise, wheels with a machined finish have a surface made up of tiny grooves (you can see them with a magnifying glass) cut into the aluminum. Machine-finished wheels have a certain character or look to them, not as shiny or as showy as fully-polished wheels, but with a more "business-like" or even a racecar look. Everyone has different tastes in wheel designs, but if you use too much abrasiveness in a cleaner on machined aluminum, those grooves can be polished down to where that original character is gone, and this may not happen evenly. Some spots may come out shinier than the rest, so use only a product recommended for that finish if you want to keep the original look of the wheels.

One aftermarket wheel which has been popular for many years on performance cars is the Centerline, and this wheel has a distinctive "brushed" finish (although some models are available from the factory in fully-polished form, too). The wheel is made of two formed sections of smooth aluminum that are riveted together, sandwiching a thick aluminum center (the lugnut area) between the two halves. If you have these wheels in their brushed-aluminum form, use a mild chemical cleaner and a very fine cleaner/wax or ultrafine polishing paste, and don't rub too hard in any one spot or the satiny look of the brushed aluminum will be lost. Some racing teams and performance car owners never use polish on brushed-aluminum wheels at all. They use fine steel wool or a fine Scotchbrite pad lubricated with WD-40. This maintains the special look of these wheels, and in fact is a technique to restore that look if you have overzealously polished such a wheel with abrasive compounds.

Older, plain cast aluminum wheels take the most work to maintain, but there is little danger of harming them with any wheel cleaner because the material is the same all the way through, not a thin surface coating. It's amazing how one of these wheels that may have been neglected for years can be brought back to life with varying grades of polishing compounds. Really neglected wheels may require starting off with fine steel wool, having soaked the steel wool first with chemical aluminum cleaner. After this initial brightening, the shine can be brought back with progressively finer grades of polish, then protected with wax. There may be holes, fasteners or other styling elements in the wheel design that require lots of painstaking work with polish applied to a rag over your fingertip. Your hands may be sore or cramped when you're done, but observers will think you opted for a new set of wheels when they see the results.

The worst-case scenario in wheel-cleaning is grappling with true magnesium wheels. These were popular on race cars and hot rods from the Fifties and Sixties, and are now sought-after collector's items. Although it is from them that "mag" wheels get their name, today the term is generic and is applied to all aftermarket wheels, which are almost always aluminum. True magnesium wheels have a special beauty when they are fully polished, like chrome but with a different cast or color to them, but the magnesium corrodes very quickly. Such wheel must be polished laboriously at least once a week to maintain their looks. If neglected for a long time, they take on a brown layer of oxidation that must be cleaned with sandpaper first, starting with 180-grit, then 320-grit, then 400, and then polished with an airtool with a small round buffing attachment and aluminum polishing rouge. Every kind of surface treatment has been tried to prolong the looks of magnesium wheels, from clear powder coats to various clear sprays, but sooner or later the gasses in the magnesium will break through these protective layers and corrosion will come in, necessitating a full-bore cleaning effort again.

Wire wheels present another tough chore in detailing, but great strides have been made in formulating new cleaners. There is a timeless elegance to a true wire wheel, but traditionally they have required considerable hand effort to clean, polishing the rim and each spoke with a cloth and chrome polish. Today there are some excellent two-step spray cleaners for chromed wire wheels. True wire wheels are quite expensive, as well as labor intensive to manufacture, and more often today we see the "wire basket" wheel, which is really a standard chromed-steel wheel with a basket of chromed spokes that attaches in the center. Unless you get up close, they look almost as good as the real thing, but there is never a problem with wheel wobble or alignment from bent or loose spokes. The basket wheels are also much easier to clean.

The better "wire wheel cleaning kits" contain a pump or spray bottle of a chemical cleaner and a second spray that neutralizes the first one for a "spray on-hose off" approach to what would otherwise be a difficult detailing task. On the wire-basket wheels, getting to the detailing baseline the first time may mean removing the wire basket section (quite easy) and cleaning and polishing the chromed wheel. The basket can be cleaned with the spray cleaners, rinsed, dried and put back on. With both true wire wheels and the basket type, a small "bottle brush" will be helpful to scrub around the spokes during the chemical cleaning, especially if there is disc brake dust present. When using any of the spray-on wheel cleaners, or when hosing them off, be sure to wear some eye protection in case of splashbacks which contain caustic chemicals.

The wire wheel look has remained popular even though factory installed wires haven't been around for decades and true wire wheels are rare even in specialty wheel circles. What you do see today are wire-look wheel covers (see illustration). These can be either chrome-plated steel, stainless-steel or plastic with plastic chrome. With the proper cleaner for the material used, these are a great deal less work to detail than true wires or even wire-basket wheels and, because they are full covers, have much less chance of being affected by brake dust.

A baseline can be achieved with most factory and aftermarket specialty wheels in one session, followed by regular, light cleaning. However, in hard-winter areas, another deep-cleaning session should take place just before the winter starts. Chromed and aluminum wheels should be thoroughly cleaned and then coated with extra wax protection, such as pure carnauba, even to the extent of protecting the backside of the wheels. Chances are you won't be doing too much wheel polishing during the depths of winter, so the extra wax will protect your aluminum and chrome from the road salts and constant moisture. Another good cleaning in spring and you're ready for the rest of the year.

11.19 True wire wheels are seldom seen anymore, even in specialty car circles. As you can imagine, they can be time-consuming to detail, but there are wire-wheel cleaning kits today that offer spray-on-hose-off convenience, although careful drying off to eliminate spots is still tedious.

11.20 Wire-wheel hubcaps are more common and can be cleaned with the same kits as real wires. The hubcaps don't get as dirty because there is a full cover behind those spokes that keeps brake dust out for the most part.

11.21 Vinylex protectant is being sprayed onto a small sponge for application, rather than spraying it on the tire which would mean overspray on your freshly-polished wheel.

Tire cleaning/protecting

Have you even gone to a paint store and asked for white paint? There must be dozens of variations of "white" paint, all differing subtly in shades, hues and intensity. You would think, on the other hand, that "black is black." There may not be many shades of black, in the paint store, but when

11.22 Using the small, square sponge allows you to get right up next to the rim when dressing the tire, with minimal effort to clean overlap from the rim when you're done.

11.23 The right look for tires in terms of glossiness is a subjective matter. After a thorough dressing of this tire, it looks a little too shiny. On neglected tires, two applications may be necessary, and the second coat may stay shiny.

11.24 After the second coat has had a chance to soak in, buff with a towel and the tire now looks more like a new one than a "painted" one.

11.25 If the tires had not been protected for a long time, dead rubber may continue to come off the tires during the dressing phase, as evidenced by this sponge and rag. The tire is quite clean now and protected.

it comes to getting a "look" for black rubber tires, there are differences. Tire rubber can be dull grey, dull black, dull brown, or any of these shades in semi-glossy or glossy, depending on the tire cleaner and dressing you use. Everyone wants their tires to look "new", but there seems to be some disagreement as to what that look is exactly.

If you have joined the "clean the wheels first" side of the tire/wheel detailing argument, you should now protect the clean wheels while you detail the tires. A tip from the people at Eagle One is to make up a cardboard disc for

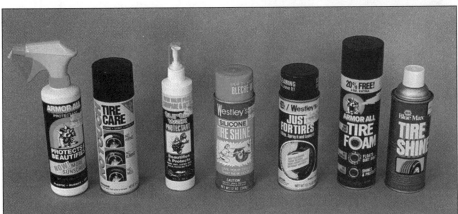

11.26 The finished wheel and tire look sparkling now, with a total effort of about 30 minutes. If regular wheel/tire maintenance is observed after this, future cleanings should take only about 5-10 minutes per corner.

11.27 There is as much commercial competition in the tire cleaner/dressing arena as there is in waxes and wheel cleaners. Once you find the brand that works best for you in terms of appearance and durability, stick with it.

11.28 Eagle One suggests making a cardboard disc and covering it with duct tape, to use as a mask when cleaning tires and wheels.

11.29 Holding the disc up to your wheel while you apply tire cleaners or dressings masks the already-cleaned wheel perfectly.

a wheel mask **(see illustrations)**. Measure the outside diameter of your wheel, noting that it is bigger than the nominal description of the wheel size (i.e. a 15-inch wheel may have an outside rim diameter over 16 inches). Put two slots in the center for hand holds and then cover the whole disc with duct tape to make it impervious to the tire cleaners and protectants. This will only work for a wheel that doesn't have a projecting center cap or spinner. There is a plastic disc made just for this purpose available in some stores, and it is domed to clear center spinners. With either device, you hold the mask up to the wheel, center it on the rim so no metal is exposed, and you can spray cleaners or protectants on the tire with no fear that it is going to necessitate recleaning the rims. Anything that does dribble in under the mask can be easily wiped off.

New tires, or tires that have been detailed since new, will require very little cleaning after the soap and brushing action from when you did your basic vehicle wash, but older or neglected tires will take some elbow grease to bring back to life. Tires tend to succumb to smog, sun and other elements much like paint, losing their suppleness, color and accumulating "dead" rubber on the surface like oxidized paint. Your detailing baseline goal with your tires is to eliminate that dead rubber, then give the tire some protectant, for gloss, color and renewed flexibility.

11.30 Tire cleaners are available specifically for whitewalls, but detailers suggest staying away from brands with bleach in them. The bleach perks up the white areas but dulls the black rubber.

11.31 It's an old-fashioned approach, but many enthusiasts still use an SOS pad to clean whitewalls. Turned on edge, the pad does a good job of scrubbing the whitewall without excessive action on the black rubber.

Some say that you can even prevent or deter sidewall cracking with regular applications of protectant, but the backside of the tire usually doesn't get the same treatment, and sidewall cracking is usually caused by low inflation pressures.

There are many varieties of tire cleaners and dressings on the market, and each has its following among enthusiasts, restorers and detailers. These are the people who should know what works best, but they all vary on their specific personal choices. Most do agree that without regular tire cleaning, continued application of oily or waxy protectants just seals dirt and dead rubber in, which can cause the tires to discolor slightly to an unattractive, brownish hue.

Tire detailing advice used to be to scrub the rubber with a brush and household scouring powder and water. Unfortunately, most such household cleaners contain bleach, which, while it can brighten up an old whitewall, will probably dull down the adjacent black part of the tire. Some of the commercial tire cleaners at your auto parts store also contain bleach, especially ones that claim to be specifically for whitewalls. There are still several well known brands of tire cleaner that do a fine job, on both the black and white parts of a tire, without the danger of changing the tire's color or staining anodized or clearcoated specialty wheels.

Scrubbing with a good tire cleaner and a stiff, short-bristled brush will do wonders for getting to your tire baseline. Some detailers use a Scotchbrite pad, which works fine for the majority of the sidewalls but is ineffective on raised lettering. For lettering, use a small, wood-handled brush with short brass bristles. Such brushes are available inexpensively at most tool stores. The brass bristles do a good job, but aren't as likely to damage the rubber details as a normal, steel wire-brush. Other detailers use an SOS pad(or steel wool with soap), particularly on whitewall stains **(see illustrations)**. A biode-

11.32 Rinse the tire thoroughly, and, as long as you get to the cleaning baseline this time, regular applications of protectant should keep both black and white areas clean.

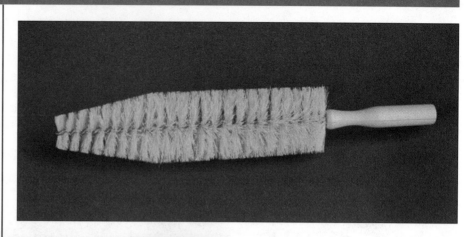

11.33 A spoke brush like this one will come in very handy when scrubbing in the details of various wheel shapes. As with any detailing brush, make sure to clean it thoroughly before putting it away so that it's ready for the next time.

gradeable household spray cleaner like Simple Green is also useful when scrubbing whitewalls. This kind of deep cleaning is necessary only to get to our baseline. Once you have cleaned the tire of dead rubber, regular applications of rubber/vinyl protectant should keep the tire from oxidizing much. You'll know you're doing a much-needed job when you see how much "soot" washes away when rinsing the tire.

After the scrubbing, rinse each tire thoroughly with clean water and let it dry completely. Examine the tires when dry for signs of streaking or discoloration. If the black areas look "healthy" and the whitewalls or white lettering is bright, you can apply protectant. Some

11.34 When a tire and wheel have been properly detailed, water should bead up there just like it does on the vehicle's paint surface. This means everything is protected from the elements and easier to clean.

11.35 No one says you have to leave your factory or aftermarket wheels as they came originally. Wheels look especially good with subtle accent areas of the wheel painted the same color as the car, although there is some tedious masking sometimes.

tire dressings are intended to be sprayed on and allowed to soak in to penetrate the rubber. If you don't have the wheel masks mentioned above, then spray the product on a clean sponge and wipe the tire thoroughly with the sponge which will do a good job of soaking the tire and not getting on your wheels. Pro detailers use an applicator for vinyl/rubber dressings. Like a large version of a shoe-polish applicator, the handle contains the liquid product, and at the end is a small, fine-cell sponge that is fed liquid anytime you invert the applicator. A similar version with a standard sponge on the end is available in some supermarkets in the "mop and brushes" aisle. The applicator is excellent for applying protectants to tires, or vinyl and rubber anywhere on the car, because it does a neat job without overspray. You can run it right around the rim area and not get any on the wheel.

Let the protectant/dressing sit on the tire for ten minutes or so. If your tire surface is already "well-fed," the protectant won't penetrate any further; if the rubber is thirsty, however, you may want to apply a second coat of protectant, especially if the first coat wasn't absorbed evenly. When the tire doesn't seem to be absorbing any more dressing, buff the tire with a terrycloth to remove excess dressing and get an even finish on the rubber.

The tire's look, in terms of color and gloss, will depend on the protectant you have used. Pro detailers and show-car owners are adamant about the particular products they like or dislike. Some protectants have a reputation for making the tires much too shiny, with an unnatural gloss that is avoided at all costs in specialty-car circles. When allowed to penetrate thoroughly, most dressings will leave too much gloss on the rubber; it's what it looks like after the buffing that counts. With some products, the tires look too glossy, but only for a day or two, after which they settle down to a "new tire" appearance. Other products have just the right look right after the rubbing. You'll just have to try a few to find the product you like best for your "color" of black. If the dressing looks too shiny, don't panic, it can easily be toned down with a little soap and water.

When you're done with this phase of detailing, you're done! By now, you have a car that looks its absolute best and is as well protected from the elements as elbow grease and chemicals can make it. From bumper to bumper, roof to rocker panels, inside and out, it is detailed, and you stand ready to bask in admiring glances and being recognized as a car-owner who takes justifiable pride in his automobile.

Notes

12

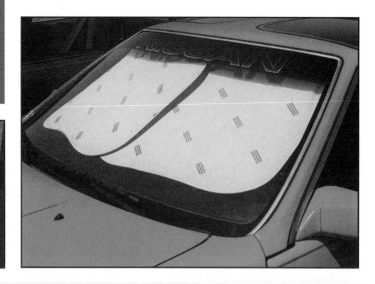

Long-term protection

12 Long-term protection

Motorists who own high-end cars are among the most concerned in doing whatever is necessary to protect their heavy investment. They also seem to take greater than average pride in their vehicle and its appearance. The rest of us can learn a great deal from their attitude. If you have read through this book so far, you now have a very clear idea of the what, why and how of detailing your car inside and out, for both looks and protection, but sometimes wax alone isn't all that can be done in the way of long-term protection.

The amount of driving you do and the road conditions you encounter most often are among the factors to consider in judging whether you need long-term protection. If you drive only 10,000 miles a year, mostly in city conditions, your concerns are different than that of the salesman or long-distance commuter who may amass 30,000 miles in that same one-year period. If you do much driving on country roads, where there is more likelihood of encountering loose gravel or driving for any period behind farm equipment or big trucks, then you should definitely consider extra protection. Even the best carnauba wax can't protect your car from flying stones, and what good is a perfectly-detailed paint job, well-cleaned, shiny and waxed, if it's peppered with chips?

12.1 When you have an expensive, rare or exotic car, extra protection in the form of a bra and car cover are a necessity, but such accessories can help maintain the appearance and value of any vehicle.

Frontal protection

One of the most common and effective extra-protection treatments for your car's exterior is a "bra" for the front end **(see illustration)**. This is the one item that will be the most valuable for those who drive higher than average annual mileage or who drive in areas where stone chips are more likely, such as on two-lane country roads. Generally made of black vinyl and cloth, a car bra or mask snaps on over the front end of your car, covering the bumper and the front ends of the hood and fenders.

Front end bras are available at automotive retail parts stores, specialty shops and through mail-order catalogs. Look through your Yellow Pages under "Auto Accessories" to find shops near you that carry them. Ads for major national companies that deal directly with consumers through 800 numbers are found in most auto

12.2 When shopping for front-end protection, make sure that you can try the mask on with a guarantee. Shown is an example of a Miatasport bra that is designed specifically for this Miata and, as such, fits perfectly. Good fit means less chance of the bra flapping and abrading the paint.

enthusiast publications. When shopping for a front end bra, look for quality in the construction and choice of materials - not all are created equal. Features to look for include: quality, heavy-weight vinyl, well-stitched seams, edges bound with soft felt, padding, reinforced areas, a soft backing material and attaching hooks that look strong and feature a soft plastic coating, cloth covering or some other kind of protection for painted surfaces.

You must shop around for a good front end bra. There are two main problems with inexpensive, poorly-manufactured bras. First, the attachment methods, which may include clips, straps, and some kind of Velcro fasteners, must be strong enough and located in the right places to both fit the car well and hold the mask on securely. You may have seen one of the lesser-quality bras flapping in the breeze on someone else's car on the freeway. Any flapping or lifting of the bra means the mask may do as much damage to the paint and chrome as it is designed to prevent. The better bras have some kind of small "spoilers" on top that make the freeway-speed airflow keep the cover down against the car, rather than lifting up **(see illustration)**. Any movement of the vinyl material against your

12.3 On this Porsche bra, note that there are Velcro-secured flaps that cover the headlights when retracted. At the top edge are two "spoilers" that are designed to keep the bra down at speed.

12.4 Bras are available for almost any vehicle, even older specialty cars. A beautiful paint job on a vintage restoration or street rod can be saved when the protection is added for long trips to car events.

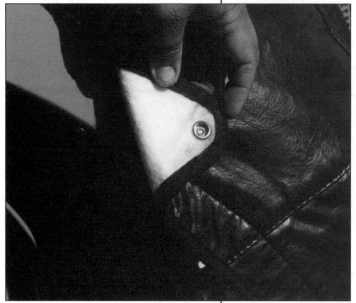

12.6 These metal tabs are made of soft metal to allow frequent bending without breaking. The tabs should be covered with plastic or padded cloth to protect your paint.

12.5 There are various methods of bra/mask attachment. This 1937 Ford has unobtrusive snaps in the fenderwell that are secure and don't flap. Other methods include bendable metal tabs covered with some kind of soft material.

paint can eventually abrade the finish.

The second problem area is fit. This is perhaps the most important consideration, and it is one you can't assess until you physically try the bra on your car. If you buy one by mail, make sure that the company offers a money-back guarantee (most good ones do). If you're buying from a store, insist that they give you a chance to try it on your car in the parking lot before you buy. A good store will not only do that but also will show you how it attaches and how to make the best use of it. The real test of how well it fits, beyond what you see as it is installed, is on the road. Try it at freeway speeds, and see how it works. If necessary, have a passenger in another car drive in the lane next to you and slightly ahead to observe how the bra behaves at speed. They should look for any loose areas flapping or any obstructions to headlights, turn signals or radiator opening.

A front end mask that fits well is styled nicely and features quality materials and construction which can take the worry out of protecting your car for the "long haul." Some drivers don't like the appearance of the bra on their vehicle,

12.7 Painted or chromed front bumpers can also be protected with a small bra available from Wardlow Top Shop.

while others think it enhances the look, particularly on the sporty models. You can decide what best suits your needs, but balance your considerations with the knowledge of what it can cost to fix a dozen or more rock chips and repaint your front end, which can be the result of not using a front end mask.

You can't just install a front end bra and forget it. If you have driven in any dusty conditions or in rain, you should remove the bra and brush or wash out dust, or trapped dirt can be ground into the paint by the cover. The bra will of course be picking up all the bug splatters that it is protecting your car from, so it should be cleaned periodically with vinyl cleaner and a brush. Hang the bra up to dry where it gets good air circulation and don't reinstall until it's perfectly dry. Treat the vinyl to some protectant after cleaning, and the next time you clean it, the bug splatters will come off a lot easier.

If you do any mechanical work on your vehicle, even to just detailing the engine compartment, you should get a vinyl fender protector or two. You have seen these in use in most auto repair shops, they are vinyl covers with a soft backing that lay over your front fender, protecting the paint from spills, dropped tools, and scratches from your belt buckle as

12.8 The bumper mask has soft backing, flexible metal tabs, and elastic-bound ends that hold it tight onto the bumper.

12.9 Front end protection for mainstream cars is available through specialty stores or through mail-order with companies advertising in car magazines. For the vintage and specialty cars, bras are often sold at swap meets and car shows.

you lean into the engine compartment **(see illustration)**. Most have a "ledge" area on top that keeps tools from rolling off, and which is also a handy place to temporarily store fasteners from whatever underhood project you're working on. They are washable, and can be helpful in protecting your fenders from chemical overspray when you are hosing off your engine after using spray degreasers. Most types have a soft foam backing that keeps them from slipping off, while some models have magnetic edges to keep them in place.

12.10 This front end mask for a 1956 Chevy features a built-in bug screen to cover the radiator/grille area. Try one of these on the road to see if the screen raises your engine temperate at all.

12.11 If you do your own mechanical work, as well as detailing, you'll want to invest in one or two vinyl fender protectors, as here on this 1954 Packard, to protect the paint on your fenders from belt buckles, shirt buttons and other abrasions when working underhood.

Side protection

Exterior protection on areas other than the front end include a variety of products designed to protect against parking-lot dings and "grocery basket rash." The best protection is well-designed factory side trim, especially with rubber inserts in the center. If your car doesn't have side trim and you're concerned about dings, aftermarket trim can be installed at any body shop. Trim is available in many sizes, styles and even colors to coordinate with your application. Some are adhesive-backed vinyl moldings that you simply cut to length and apply, following a straight and level line you have drawn on the car with washable grease pencil. Other types have a more factory look to them, with metal moldings and vinyl rub strips in the center. The latter type usually requires drilling holes in the body, using "pop" rivets to attach the metal channels and then inserting the vinyl center strips. Some are flexible, one-piece moldings that have chromed plastic

12.12 The rear edge of your door can be protected with a slip-on vinyl or metal edge-guard like this. It sticks out beyond your factory side trim, in case you open your door and hit another object.

edges to appear like traditional metal moldings.

In addition to side trim, there are accessory edge-trim pieces that protect the rear edges of your doors **(see illustration)**. Your local auto parts store should have several types, including metal U-channel trim you cut to length and tap in place on the rear edge of your door with a rubber hammer. These can be colored plastic, chromed plastic or metal (aluminum, chromed steel, or stainless-steel). Such door guards offer protection only from your door being chipped as you open it, perhaps tapping the car next to you. They don't protect from someone else opening their door against your car.

Similar to door edge trim is fender trim. These are usually chromed or gold-anodized aluminum and attach all around the inside edge of your fenderwell. They simulate the look of more expensive cars that have such trim as standard equipment, and many car owners put this fender trim on more for the looks than the paint protection. Such trim can often be ordered dealer-installed when you buy a new car, giving you the "expensive look" as an option even if you're buying a lesser-priced model. Some of the fender trims are cut-to-fit universal types, while others are shaped particularly for specific model cars. Almost all fender-edge trim requires drilling and riveting the trim to the inner lip of the fenderwell, but, unlike side moldings, if you decide to remove the fender trim at some later point the rivets can be drilled out and the holes aren't noticeable unless you look under the fender.

Protection of the rocker panels and bottom of the rear quarter-panels is available in the form of mudflaps **(see illustration)**. These have been around for many years and can do a good job of keeping mud and rocks from being thrown

12.13 Mudflaps have been around since before the automobile was invented, and they are still a viable way of keeping mud and stones from ruining your rocker panels and rear quarter panels.

12.14 If your vehicle sees long-term outdoor storage, you may want to protect the tires from rain and UV exposure with simple tire covers as shown on this boat trailer. Covers are available at most RV supply stores.

12.15 Floormats are an inexpensive investment in protecting the area of your interior subject to the most wear and tear.

up by the wheels onto your paint. As with the fender trim, there are those car owners who don't like the look of mudflaps and others who put them on just because of the way they look. Another similarity shared with the fender-edge trim is that removing the mudflaps, which typically attach to the inside edge of the fenderwell with a few small screws, is easy and doesn't leave visible damage to the outside of the car.

Interior protection

The abrasion of the outdoor elements on your paint is almost matched by the punishment taken by your interior, particularly the carpeting and driver's seat, areas where ounces of prevention can be worth pounds in additional resale value. There is no bigger giveaway of high mileage on a vehicle than the condition of the driver's seat. If the material is worn, frayed and heavily soiled, neither a private party nor a dealer is going to give you anything above the "low bluebook" value for your car when you sell or trade. A neglected paint job can often be "rescued" with the proper detailing materials and elbow grease, but saving upholstery beyond the cleaning instructions we have given you so far is a matter for an upholsterer, who has to replace worn material at considerable expense.

Carpeting is commonly protected with accessory floormats. There was a time, 20 years or more ago, when carpeting in an automobile was considered an option, and the base vehicles all had rubber floorcovering, but today even the small cars are factory carpeted. Most cars come equipped with some kind of over-the-carpet protection as well. You'll find accessory floormats in two basic styles and enough different colors that a close match can be made with most factory interiors **(see illustration)**. Almost all are made of colored rubber with carpeting on top, and usually have little "gripper" spike on the bottom to keep them in place on your original carpeting. There are mats which cover your carpet-

12.16 After a few years of driving, you may start to see minor wear on your seats and want to protect them from further dirt and abrasion with seat covers. The suede leather in this car is difficult to maintain, so covers will be used.

12.17 You'll find a variety of seat covers colors, materials and designs to choose from at your auto supply store, from universal-fit to custom sheepskin covers.

12.18 Before slipping the seat cover on, the headrest must be removed. Some have a release button, but on this Pontiac a thin hacksaw blade must be inserted along the front edge of the post, pushing back the detents so the headrest can be removed.

ing from doorsill to doorsill, covering even the drive-line tunnel of the floor. Such mats are often tailored for specific vehicles and offer maximum protection of the original carpeting. Less expensive and more universal are the mats that cover only the floor area where your feet most often contact your carpeting. Because they are only modified squares or rectangles in shape, they can fit just about any vehicle and are easy to remove to clean the accessory mats and the stock carpeting underneath. After floormats have been in place a long time, your factory carpeting may become matted down and pocked with "holes" from the placeholding spikes on the back of the accessory mats, but a little work with shampoo and a carpet brush will bring the nap right back up, and in fact this should be done a few times a year.

Protecting the seats in your interior is not as unobtrusively done as with the carpeting. Seat covers are the only way to save your upholstery from wear and dirt, and covers are quite obvious. What's available in seat coverings ranges from cheap, thin terrycloth covers that are universal-fit to expensive, genuine-sheepskin covers made for specific sports-model and luxury-car seats. In between are seat covers styled much like your original upholstery (yet still obviously not stock) and imitation sheepskin covers that are more universal than the expensive ones. Universality in seat covers means that the cover may fit your seat nicely, or it may

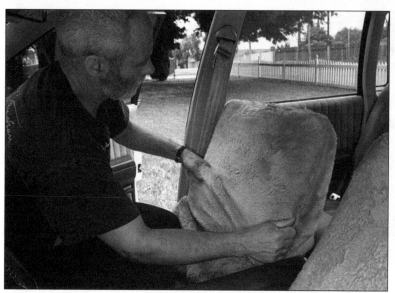

12.19 Work the seatcover down over the seat, trying to get the wrinkles out as you go. The better the fit of the cover, the harder to install.

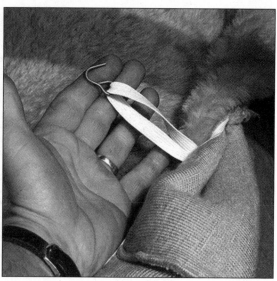

12.20 Most inexpensive covers have elastic straps and S-hooks all around the bottom for attachment to your stock seat frame.

not. Most seat covers are supplied with stretchy straps and S-shaped metal hooks for installation **(see illustrations)**. You pull the cover over your seat, tighten the straps and attach the hooks under the seat to the springs or frame. Sometimes a little creativity in attachment (like making extra mounting points) of an inexpensive seatcover can go a long way toward making it look more like it was made for your car. Loose seatcovers can be annoying because you can slide around on the seat, and when you're not in the car the cheaper covers can be bunched up on one side of the seat, creating an untidy appearance.

Compared to full reupholstery at a professional shop, seatcovers are an inexpensive method of "fixing up" a used

12.21 Pull the cover material as tight against the seat as you can, and reach as far under the seat to find an attachment as is necessary to keep tension on the cover so it won't slide around on the original upholstery.

12.22 After seatcover installation, the headrest can be reinserted. Usually, covers are not available for headrests, but you can attach a clean white terrycloth face towel over the headrest for stain protection and pin it with safety pins.

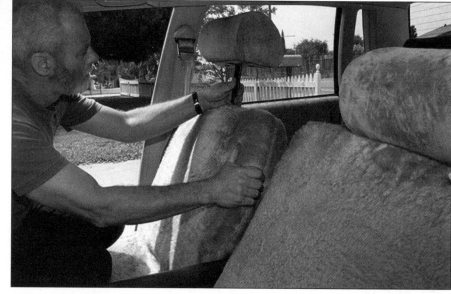

Long-term protection

12.23 Inexpensive sunshields are available universally, like these cloth ones mounted on a flexible wire frame. They twist up into a small circle for storage.

car you may have purchased that has torn or deteriorated seats. Not every motorist likes the look of them in a new car, however. They can protect your upholstery, but some drivers would rather enjoy the beauty and "integrated" look of the factory interior, at least for the first three or four years of ownership, and only then start to think about covers as the seats begin showing extra wear.

With the increasing amount of glass area in today's cars, ultraviolet light is a bigger factor than ever in the

12.24 At better car accessory stores, higher-quality sunshields are available made with cardboard stiffeners covered with UV-resistant material. They fold up when not in use.

fading and deterioration of a vehicle's interior. Seat coverings and floor mats can protect those areas, but the dashboard and rear "package shelf" areas have probably the greatest exposure to the UV rays through the large, sloping windshield and rear window. Such constant exposure on sunny days is the main cause of cracking in vinyl-covered dashboards, and the UV can also damage the topmost upholstery of the rear seat as well as the cloth or vinyl covering of the package shelf directly under the back window.

Prevention of interior fading due to UV exposure is one of the main reasons for window tinting, whether factory or aftermarket. The tinting also changes the 'look' of the vehicle and keeps the interior cooler, but should be considered as an excellent preventative measure in protecting your interior.

Even with window tinting, which by law in many states is illegal on the windshield and front door glass, there is still considerable exposure of the dash area. One solution is the sunshield (see illustrations). You have all seen inexpensive cardboard versions of these in cars in parking lots. The folded cardboard, often with an advertising message on one side and a "Help, Police!" sign on the other, is set up between the windshield and the dash, usually kept in place by your sun visors and rear-view mirror. Inexplicably, so many motorists have been using them incorrectly for years, always displaying the "call for help" sign whenever

12.25 Edge-bound carpet dashcovers are a popular sun-country accessory, protecting the vinyl dash from cracking and keeping it non-glare.

12.26 Better-quality dashcovers are made to fit each specific vehicle and feature colors to coordinate with factory interiors. Velcro strips keep them in place.

they park, that the original secondary use of the sunshield as an emergency aid is largely negated. However, whatever side you display, these inexpensive shields (sometimes given away by the advertiser as a promotion) do help keep your interior cooler and protect the dash from UV rays, at least while you are parked. For a few dollars more, there are better-made versions of the sunshields with UV-resistant vinyl material (often of a reflective color like silver or gold for even greater heat protection for the interior) over cardboard stiffeners, with a soft felt on the other side. These are usually more model-specific than universal in dimensions.

Another method of dash protection is a dashcover or dashguard. The terminology is applied loosely in the marketplace to a variety of products, but there are covers that are made of the same ABS plastic as your dashboard, with the same colors and texture, that attach with adhesive or Velcro and become like a "second skin" to your original dash. Such covers are ideal for renewing the look of an interior whose dash is already showing hideous cracks, with some designs hard to tell from an OEM (Original Equipment Manufacture) dash.

Other options for protecting your good, original dash are covers or "guards" made of molded and edge-bound carpeting **(see illustration)**. These are available from a number of manufacturers, with varying degrees of exactness to their fit on your specific car. Some are designed to loosely sit on the dash only when you are parked, while others have Velcro attachments and are molded to fit your dash contours. Another benefit of the carpet-type covers is reducing the glare that can come from the stock dash, even a "semi-gloss" vinyl dash. For some vehicles, fabric dashboard sunshields are available that not only cover the dash directly under the windshield but also are shaped to cover the steering wheel and hang down over the instrument panel.

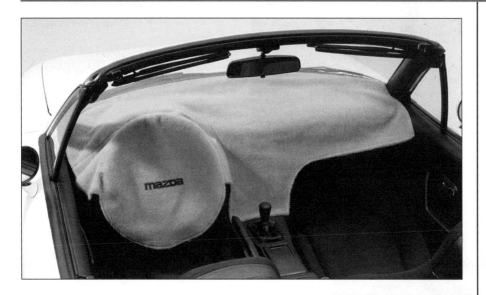

12.27 Sometimes you can find a dashcover, like this Miatasport item for the Miata, that also covers the steering wheel to keep it cool and protected, especially important on a convertible.

They can keep the steering wheel from getting hot and/or deteriorating from UV exposure. They also keep your dash-mounted stereo components from view, something to consider if you must leave your car in a parking lot for a long period.

The steering wheel itself can be easily protected with a tie-on or lace-on steering-wheel cover. These are available in stores and specialty catalogs. Inexpensive steering wheel covers are made of foam or light vinyl and slip over the stock wheel, while better ones are made of premium vinyl or even leather and attach by lacing around the inside circumference of the wheel. These have the most OEM look. Though they do offer excellent protection, steering wheel covers are more often used to cosmetically cover a wheel showing lots of wear, or to give a softer grip to an older, non-cushioned wheel, than to simply protect a new wheel from wear and dirt.

12.28 A quality car cover is a worthwhile investment for any valuable car that must spend a lot of time outdoors and in the sun.

Car covers

Besides storage in a clean, dry, heated garage, there is probably no better method of extended car protection than a good car cover because it provides insurance in several areas at once **(see illustrations)**. While it's main function in good weather is to protect the car from UV exposure (protecting the paint, interior, bumpers, tires and other exterior rubber), it also protects a convertible when the top is down and provides a measure of secrecy and security when it comes to theft of your stereo or even the whole car. A good cover keeps dust off all your surfaces and protects paint, glass and chrome from tree sap, acid rain, bird droppings, wind-blown sand, etc., and the thicker ones even offer some protection

12.29 The design of a good, multi-layer car cover is such that moisture from inside can escape and not be trapped on the car, but the cover resists exterior moisture, such as morning dew, from coming in. Higher-protection covers are made for extended use in inclement weather.

12.30 The inexpensive plastic car covers sold in the discount stores are OK for an occasional use to protect from airborne materials, but they usually don't fit any car well and can trap moisture inside.

from runaway shopping carts and kids on bikes.

Choosing the brand of car cover will be tougher than using one. The cheap, plastic ones sold in some discount stores are not helpful to a plan of extended car protection, they are only useful in a short emergency (like protection from airborne ash deposits, painting oversprays or fallout from government insect spraying). Used on a regular basis, such covers can cause mildew to form inside and around your vehicle because the plastic can't "breathe" and consequently traps moisture inside. With little air movement between the atmosphere and the car under the cover, the car can get even hotter than ambient temperature rather than cooler.

Discounting the plastic covers, you have several leading names in quality car cover manufacturing, each with extensive advertising and experience in the field, but with different approaches to the construction and materials they feel a car cover should be made from. They all agree a good car cover should "breathe" but disagree on the best material for the job. Some are in the all-cotton camp; others promote man-made materials such as Evolution 3 polypropylene fabric from Kimberly-Clark, or even "polycotton" material which is a blend of 50/50 to 60/40 polyester-to-cotton fabric.

The available covers range from the unlined cotton or polycotton to a more expensive type which uses the same material outside but is lined with very soft flannel on the in-

12.31 The advantage of the plastic covers is that they fold up really small for storage, and this one comes with an attached bag to fold it into.

12.32 Look for double-stitched seams on any car cover you buy, as well as a performance and fit guarantee.

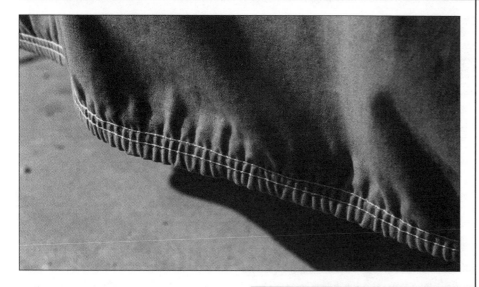

12.33 Elastic sewn in around the bottom edges of the cover helps keep the cover fitting closer to your vehicle's contours and secures it to the car during windy periods.

side. There are also the three and four-layer man-made materials and a newer synthetic material described as "space-age" that is quite expensive. The first group, the unlined cotton and polycotton covers, are fine for most uses. The material breathes enough to let moisture out of the car while not letting rain in. To a degree, these covers are resistant to water, but they are not intended for long-term outside storage of a car in inclement weather. Mildew can get a foothold on any material, given the right conditions of warmth and moisture. Most of the quality car covers on the market are treated with 3M Scotchgard for resistance to stains and dirt, and are at the same time machine-washable.

12.34 Most car covers have clearly marked fronts, usually where the manufacturer puts its logo. It's helpful, therefore, to look for the logo when putting the cover on.

The next price level in car covers brings you to the lined cotton or polycotton types which are thicker for more protection against parking-lot dings. Their inside surfaces are the ultimate in softness which is ideal for cars with delicate or special paintjobs.

The various higher-end covers using the Evolution 3 and Evolution 4 fabrics in a three-layer or four-layer car cover offer greatly increased resistance to the effects of weather. The material is very light in weight, remains flexible even in cold weather and is said not to smell, rot or be subject to formation of mildew. Although the material can "breathe," it is more resistant to tears, punctures and accidental chemical spills than cotton or polycotton and can even be used in snow conditions.

The upper-end in car covers consists of those with a new, space-age outer material layer sandwiched with a foam center layer and an inside layer of soft cotton. The new material is very light, yet is the most resistant to water, salt air, smog and dust. It has "microscopic" pores that let air through, but keep water out. Such protection doesn't come cheap - these covers are more than twice the cost of a plain cotton or polycotton cover - but they offer the ultimate protection. You'll have to decide what is best for you, based on when, where and how often you keep your car covered.

Among the performance characteristics to look for in choosing a car cover are: mildew resistance, fade resistance and water repellency. Look for quality

12.35 When you take the folded cover out of the trunk, place it at the front edge of the hood and start unrolling it to the rear.

12.36 With the whole cover rolled out lengthwise, you can now pull the cover over each side. Reverse the procedure to take the cover off, pull up the sides toward the centerline of the car and roll up the cover from back to front.

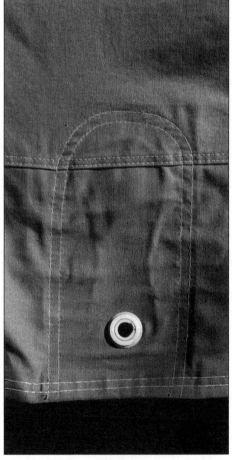

12.37 A cover that really covers your car helps to protect not only the interior, glass and paint surfaces, but also the wheel and tires. It also offers a certain protection from small parking-lot dings and scratches and gives an expensive specialty car a "lower profile" for security.

12.38 Quality covers usually come with a special reinforced section on each side around the midpoint of the car for attaching a cord to secure the cover against wind.

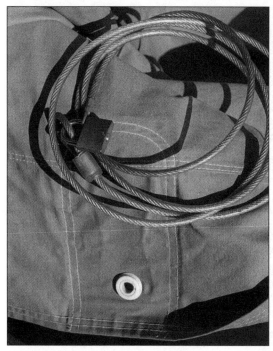

12.39 A steel cable and small padlock are offered as an option by some car cover companies as a "security package."

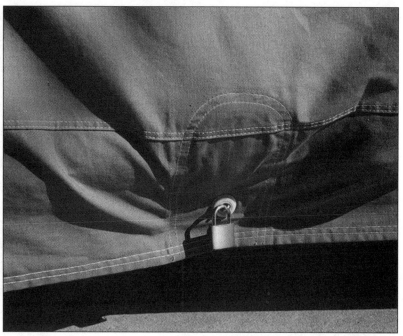

12.40 With the steel cable looped through both sides of the cover (underneath the car) and secured with the padlock, the cover won't blow away, and it keeps the overly-curious from examining your car and its contents too closely.

construction details such as the fit to your specific vehicle, double-stitched over-lapped seams, neoprene elastic sewn into the corners front and rear, machine-washability, Scotchgard treatment, and pre-shrunk or no-shrink materials throughout **(see illustrations)**. There are also options when it comes to ordering a cover. If you have special requirements that make the shape of your car slightly different than the standard model, such as an add-on luggage rack on the roof or trunk, a ski rack, larger aftermarket brush guards or some other customized feature, the bigger car-cover companies can custom-build one to suit your needs by modifying their standard pattern for your make and model. You can tell them where your antenna is located and have them sew in a reinforced grommet there. Most cover companies also offer a standard option of a plastic-covered steel cable and lock that can be used to secure the cover on your car to prevent theft of the cover**(see illustrations)**.

Special protection for trucks

Because of the loads they carry, the constant loading and unloading and the kinds of places a truck can be driven, extra protection is often in order. Although they are not as easy to find as passenger car masks, a few companies have bras produced specifically for trucks. There are also clear plastic headlight covers, bug deflectors, and you may even find a vinyl cover that is made just to protect your front bumper.

The clear plastic headlight covers are helpful when driving in conditions where stone chips are likely. Even small rocks can shatter a headlight lens, and, at the cost of replacement halogen headlights today, these covers can pay for themselves rapidly. In some states, headlight covers may not be legal when the headlights need to be on (i.e. at night) because of DMV concerns that the covers will diffuse light and reduce headlight performance, but it is rare to see a citation given out for having such covers.

12.41 Trucks have special needs for extra protection. These plastic wind and bug deflectors help keep a lot of rocks, sand and bug splatters off your windshield when driving in dusty or agricultural areas.

12.42 Trucks, even older trucks, can be fitted with front end bras for further front-end protection for quality paint jobs.

12.43 Inside your truck, you can protect the carpeting in your extended cab with one of the plastic accessory storage shelves for tapes, maps, tools, flashlight and other items that might otherwise roll around.

When shopping for front end masks for trucks, see if there is a model that incorporates a plastic screen material over the grille area, instead of just being open. On country roads, wherever there are agricultural fields or farm animals, there are lots of flying insects, which can really make a mess of your carefully-detailed grille, not to mention the reduction in cooling system performance when the radiator is fully plastered with their remains. The bras with screens can be washed out with a scrub-brush periodically, with less labor than cleaning inside your grille bars. Test such a bra on your truck and watch the temperature gauge. Depending on the mesh, the screen material can block a little airflow to the radiator, perhaps

Long-term protection

12.44 Stores that sell camper shells for trucks are a good source for extra-protection items and accessories.

raising the engine's operating temperature by 5 to 10 degrees. If your vehicle can't handle this, return the cover or exchange it for one with no screen.

Other areas of trucks that need protection are the large, outside rearview mirrors and the front edge of big rear fenders (as on "dually" trucks). The outside mirrors are usually chromed steel or stain-

12.45 Simple truckbed protection ranges from a piece of old carpeting cut to fit your truck, to rubber mats which clean up easily and offer more impact protection than carpeting. This one is called the "Fat Mat" because of its thickness.

12.46 There are shops around the country that offer sprayed-on truckbed liners. It looks like a plastic or rubber truck liner when done, but is sprayed in placed to fit all your truck's contours. Obviously, it doesn't come out for cleaning.

12.47 Standard truckbed liners are molded of strong black plastic to fit various popular pick-ups. At left is the "below-the-rail" type, at right the "over-the-rail" type. The former is used when there is a camper shell to be put over the bed.

less-steel, both of which clean up easily with standard cleaners, polishes and waxes, but there are mirror covers available with an elastic edge that slips around the leading side of most mirrors to keep stones and bug splatters off the mirrors. On the lower-front area of dually rear fenders, you can install chromed, sheetmetal decorative panels in the most vulnerable area. Since most of the dually rear fenders are fiberglass, they are particularly vulnerable to damage from flying stones. If you can't find a ready-made panel to attach for protection, you can make a cardboard template of the area you need to cover and simply cut out a protector from a chromed (thin sheetmetal) mudflap, attaching it with rivets or screws. Another solution, somewhat less effective than the metal, is to paint those areas of the fenders with a thick, rubberized paint. For this to blend in, your regular vehicle color coat should be painted over the rubberized paint, which is designed to absorb impact and let stones bounce off.

The cargo area of trucks large and small takes the most punishment. In the truck bed itself, shifting loads will sooner or later cause scrapes and dents to the painted bed. If you use your truck only for small loads once in a great while, you can cut a bed mat out of household carpeting that does a fairly good job of protecting the bed from scrapes and spilled liquids. New or used carpet remnants can be purchased inexpensively. Some carpet stores will sell you a piece of "takeout" carpet, something they have just removed from a house or office, at a bargain price if you don't need brand new, designer carpet. When cutting the carpeting, leave the length about two feet longer than the bed, so you can turn up the front edge to cover the vertical part of the bed just behind the cab. This extra protection at the front can prevent shifting loads from damaging the front of the bed.

Truck accessory shops, and even many new-vehicle dealerships, sell bed-liners which are molded plastic "inserts" that fit into your truck bed (see illustration). Usually sold with a companion piece of plastic to cover the inside of the tailgate, the liners cover all of the bed, including the sides and front, and have ribs molded in for strength. At dealerships they can often be added on as a dealer option when purchasing a new truck. Bedliners can add to the resale value of a truck, not only because they protect the bed, but also because most prospective truck buyers would want the bedliner themselves. Prices and quality vary on bedliners - shop for one with heavy-duty materials and a guarantee.

12.48 Camper stores also have these carpeted bedliners that go together in three section, come out easily for cleaning and feature bench seating and storage bins.

Long-term protection

12.49 Tonneau covers, of soft vinyl and hard fiberglass, are also available for protection and security of items in your truckbed if you don't have a shell.

Also at the rear of a truck, tailgate edges can take a beating, from lumber loaded on top, to the constant abrasion caused by the rubber weatherstrip at the bottom edge of a camper shell's back hatch. For both situations, the solution is a plastic

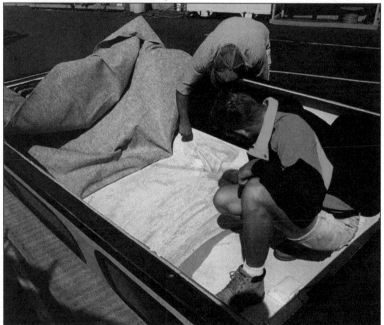

12.50 One of the custom features being offered now on camper shells is a custom-fit headliner that really details the inside of the shell. Very sticky contact cement is spread around the overturned shell, and the material is pressed into place and trimmed.

12.51 Shells can be purchased with the lining already in them, or the camper store can install the material in your own shell. It makes the interior look better inside than just raw fiberglass and is quieter and more insulated for camping.

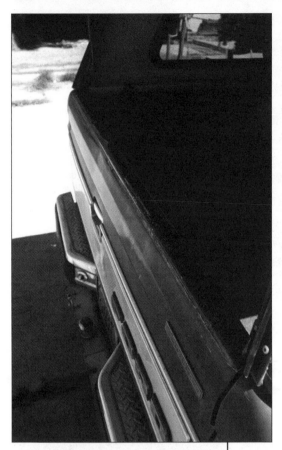

12.52 The upper edge of a truck's tailgate can take a beating from constant loading and unloading, as evidenced by the scratched paint here.

12.53 Accessory tailgate protectors are a good idea for protecting a new truck as well as fixing up an older truck by covering up previous damage.

or metal tailgate protector. Usually chromed or stainless metal, they are U-shaped channels that fit snugly over the upper edge of the tailgate, where they both protect the paint and dress up the tailgate a little **(see illustration)**.

Your detailing "kit"

If all of the detailing tips and techniques we have discussed so far in this book are used only once, you will have enhanced the beauty and value of your vehicle, but for how long? Detailing is a continuing process, not a one-time task.

12.54 It's very convenient to carry all your detailing supplies in your trunk in one of these plastic tote-trays, keeping the supplies together and preventing spillage in your trunk.

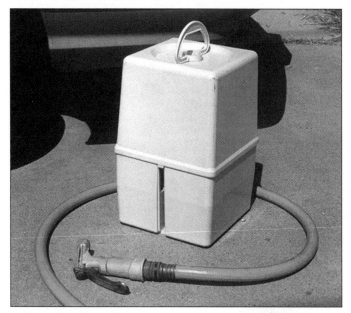

12.55 The Porta-Maid is a detailing tool for organizing all of your supplies in a handy, enclosed form.

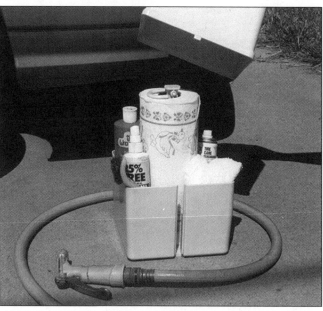

12.56 Turn the top handle, remove the cover and you see the storage area for supplies and a roll of paper towels.

Done right, by first getting to the base-lines we have described, and then maintaining that great look with consistent "housekeeping," it will make your car a source of pride for as long as you care to own it. There are many 20 and 30-year-old cars in strictly-original condition that show at concours events all the time, and have the detailed looks to win awards. They haven't retained their like-new looks over the years because of some miracle "Teflon-coating" wax or because they've been kept hermetically-sealed in a time capsule - lots of caring elbow grease and attention to detail keeps them show-ready.

After the hard work of getting to the baseline, future detailing should be

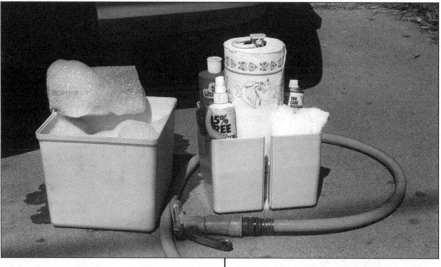

12.57 The top now becomes a 1.5-gallon wash bucket, and the bottom dispenses paper towels, solving the problem of the ever-rolling-away towel roll.

greatly simplified - dirt comes off much easier from surfaces treated with cleaners, waxes and protectants. This is not to say that a bottle of "five-minute" detailer is all you'll ever need from now on, but you now have and are familiar with all of the products and processes. Keeping up with detailing maintenance is made less of a chore if you organize your detailing materials into a "kit" **(see illustration)**.

Kept in your trunk, a detailing kit can be simple or involved, but having everything handy makes it much more likely that you will continue detailing rather than let things slide because you're too busy to round up all the necessary stuff from the garage. Make that part easy, and you won't have an excuse!

Obviously, you can't keep one of everything in your trunk or you'd have to heave your spare tire and jack, but the most important items should be there. At the very least you should have paper towels, clean cotton towels, cleaner/wax, glass cleaner and vinyl cleaner and protectant. Beyond those basic products, it would be helpful to have several scrub brushes, wash mitt, container of car-washing soap and a clean plastic bucket. The bucket can be used to corral all the other products, but you should find a method of keeping the bucket upright in the trunk so the contents aren't pitched out, perhaps to spill, on the first hard corner.

If you have room, the next level up in a kit would be to add a spray bottle of clear water, a chamois and sponge, chrome cleaner and wheel cleaner. The spray bottle of water is extremely helpful in dealing with minor emergencies like interior spills or bird droppings on the paint. If such problems can be easily addressed right after they happen, the consequences to fabric and paint will be minimal.

Plastic "tote" trays and inexpensive toolboxes are ideal for keeping all your detailing supplies together. The beauty of these over using the washbucket as a toolbox is that once the bucket is in use, all your supplies are now scattered, while the tote tray can be carried around to whatever part of the vehicle you're working on. If you're detailing the left front, you don't have to make several trips to the trunk for something else you discovered you needed.

One item that we have used that is really helpful in the trunk is the Porta-Maid. This is a plastic container that has a top and bottom half which come apart with a twist of a knob on top. The top section now becomes a 1.5-gallon wash bucket, while the bottom half holds a roll of paper towel plus brushes and cleaning supplies. This is something a detailer must have designed.

Many more ideas for detailing and car care products and tools you didn't even know you needed can be found in mail-order catalogs like those from Griot's Garage and the Eastwood Company (see Sourcelist). Specialty tools, paints, cleaning products, brushes made specifically for detailing, and much more is available if you want to carry your new interest in car care further.

For some, detailing becomes a kind of passion, closely allied with a love of automobiles, and in fact that love of cars is probably a prerequisite for following

the detailing path much beyond the basics. You have to appreciate the clarity of image in line and color that comes only from a paint job that has been "massaged," the feel of a great leather seat that is ten years old but still feels as supple as new, the mirror quality of a bumper well-protected from the elements or the pleasure of a routine oil check on an engine that is spotless.

If none of that sounds important to you and your car is no more or less than a transportation device you'd like to protect as an investment, this book is still for you. However far you eventually carry the detailing process and whatever you're driving, daily grocery-getter or concours-winner, we hope that this book has given you the methods, materials and inspiration.

12.58 One final detailing product you can keep in the trunk is a car duster. Various makes of these can be found in auto parts stores, and some are heavily advertised on television. The mop-like fibers are treated with a special wax that attracts dust. Many a car wash has been avoided by running the duster lightly over the whole car.

Sourcelist

Sourcelist

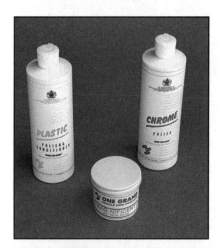

American Clean Car
500 N. Dearborn Street
Chicago, IL 60610-9988
car wash trade magazine

American Plastic Chrome
1398 Marann
Westland, MI 48185
chrome-plating of plastic parts

Auto Laundry
Columbia Communications
370 Lexington Avenue
New York, NY 10017
carwash trade magazine

Beverly Hills Motoring Accessories
200 S. Robertson Blvd.
Beverly Hills, CA 90211
car covers

Boyd's Wheels, Inc.
8380 Cerritos Avenue
Stanton, CA 90680
car-care products

California Car Cover Company
21125 Superior Street
Chatsworth, CA 91311
car covers, car dusters

Clean-Rite Products
600 Wharton Cr. SW
P.O. Box 43526
Atlanta, GA 30336
brushes, sponges, detailing accessories

Colgan Custom Manufacturing
18475 Bandilier Circle
Fountain Valley, CA 92708-7012
front end bras and car covers

Covercraft Industries, Inc.
100 Enterprise Boulevard
Pauls Valley, OK 73075
car covers

DashHugger
15345 Bonanza Drive
Victorville, CA 92392
tailored dash covers

D&D Plastic Chrome Plating
6484 Edgewater
Erie, MI 48133
chroming of plastic and fiberglass

The Eastwood Company
580 Lancaster Ave., Box 3014
Malvern, PA 19355-0714
mail-order catalog of tools, restoration and detailing supplies

Mr. G's Rechromed Plastic
5613 Elliott Reeder Rd.
Ft. Worth, TX 76117
plastic repairs and chroming

Griot's Garage
3500-A 20th St. E.
Tacoma, WA 98424
mail-order catalog of tools and detailing supplies

Hemmings Motor News
P.O. Box 1108
Bennington, VT 05201
monthly magazine of collector-car classified ads and resources

Hobby Club USA
10771 Monte Vista
Ontario, CA 91762
Dazy Spray bottle

Jet-Hot Coatings
1-800-432-3379
Arizona, Mississippi, Pensylvania
high-temp exhaust coatings

Lexol, Div. of Summit Industries
839 Pickens Industrial Drive
P.O. Box 7329
Marietta, GA 30062-3100
leather and vinyl-care products

Made For You Products
P.O. Box 720700
Pinon Hills, CA 92372
Porta-Maid™ detailing box/bucket

Meguiar's, Inc.
17991 Mitchell South
P.O. Box 17177
Irvine, CA 92713
full line of show-quality detailing products

Metro Molded Parts, Inc.
11610 Jay Street
P.O. Box 33130
Minneapolis, MN 55433
restoration rubber parts

Miatasport
1139 W. Collins Avenue
Orange, CA 92667
Mazda Miata accessories

Mother's
5456 Industrial Drive
Huntington Beach, CA 92649
full line of show-quality detailing products

Motorsport Auto
1139 W. Collins Avenue
Orange, CA 92667
Nissan "Z" accessories

National Parts Depot
1376 Walker Street, #1
Ventura, CA 93003
restoration supplies for Mustangs, T-Bird, Camaro, and Chevelle

One Grand Products
1645-C Lemonwood Drive
Santa Paula, CA 93060
full line of professional detailing supplies

Professional Carwash and Detail
National Trade Publications
13 Century Hill Drive
Latham, NY 12110-2197
trade magazine

Wardlow Top Shop
2680 Atlantic Avenue
Long Beach, CA 90806
custom front end masks, masks for older vehicles

Index

Haynes Automotive Detailing Manual

Index

HAYNES AUTOMOTIVE MANUALS

NOTE: New manuals are added to this list on a periodic basis. If you do not see a listing for your vehicle, consult your local Haynes dealer for the latest product information.

ACURA

*1776   **Integra & Legend** all models '86 thru '90

AMC

  Jeep CJ - see *JEEP* (412)
694   **Mid-size models,** Concord, Hornet, Gremlin & Spirit '70 thru '83
934   **(Renault) Alliance & Encore** all models '83 thru '87

AUDI

615   **4000** all models '80 thru '87
428   **5000** all models '77 thru '83
1117   **5000** all models '84 thru '88

AUSTIN

  Healey Sprite - see *MG Midget Roadster* (265)

BMW

*2020   **3/5 Series** not including diesel or all-wheel drive models '82 thru '92
276   **320i** all 4 cyl models '75 thru '83
632   **528i & 530i** all models '75 thru '80
240   **1500 thru 2002** all models except Turbo '59 thru '77
348   **2500, 2800, 3.0 & Bavaria** all models '69 thru '76

BUICK

  Century (front wheel drive) - see *GENERAL MOTORS* (829)
*1627   **Buick, Oldsmobile & Pontiac Full-size (Front wheel drive)** all models '85 thru '93
  Buick Electra, LeSabre and Park Avenue; Oldsmobile Delta 88 Royale, Ninety Eight and Regency; Pontiac Bonneville
1551   **Buick Oldsmobile & Pontiac Full-size (Rear wheel drive)**
  Buick Estate '70 thru '90, Electra '70 thru '84, LeSabre '70 thru '85, Limited '74 thru '79
  Oldsmobile Custom Cruiser '70 thru '90, Delta 88 '70 thru '85, Ninety-eight '70 thru '84
  Pontiac Bonneville '70 thru '81, Catalina '70 thru '81, Grandville '70 thru '75, Parisienne '83 thru '86
627   **Mid-size Regal & Century** all rear-drive models with V6, V8 and Turbo '74 thru '87
  Regal - see *GENERAL MOTORS* (1671)
  Skyhawk - see *GENERAL MOTORS* (766)
552   **Skylark** all X-car models '80 thru '85
  Skylark '86 on - see *GENERAL MOTORS* (1420)
  Somerset - see *GENERAL MOTORS* (1420)

CADILLAC

*751   **Cadillac Rear Wheel Drive** all gasoline models '70 thru '92
  Cimarron - see *GENERAL MOTORS* (766)

CAPRI

296   **2000 MK I Coupe** all models '71 thru '75
  Mercury Capri - see *FORD Mustang* (654)

CHEVROLET

*1477   **Astro & GMC Safari Mini-vans** '85 thru '93
554   **Camaro V8** all models '70 thru '81
866   **Camaro** all models '82 thru '92
  Cavalier - see *GENERAL MOTORS* (766)
  Celebrity - see *GENERAL MOTORS* (829)
625   **Chevelle, Malibu & El Camino** all V6 & V8 models '69 thru '87
449   **Chevette & Pontiac T1000** '76 thru '87
550   **Citation** all models '80 thru '85

*1628   **Corsica/Beretta** all models '87 thru '92
274   **Corvette** all V8 models '68 thru '82
*1336   **Corvette** all models '84 thru '91
1762   **Chevrolet Engine Overhaul Manual**
704   **Full-size Sedans** Caprice, Impala, Biscayne, Bel Air & Wagons '69 thru '90
  Lumina - see *GENERAL MOTORS* (1671)
  Lumina APV - see *GENERAL MOTORS* (2035)
319   **Luv Pick-up** all 2WD & 4WD '72 thru '82
626   **Monte Carlo** all models '70 thru '88
241   **Nova** all V8 models '69 thru '79
*1642   **Nova and Geo Prizm** all front wheel drive models, '85 thru '92
420   **Pick-ups '67 thru '87** - Chevrolet & GMC, all V8 & in-line 6 cyl, 2WD & 4WD '67 thru '87; Suburbans, Blazers & Jimmys '67 thru '91
*1664   **Pick-ups '88 thru '93** - Chevrolet & GMC, all full-size (C and K) models, '88 thru '93
*831   **S-10 & GMC S-15 Pick-ups** all models '82 thru '92
*1727   **Sprint & Geo Metro** '85 thru '91
*345   **Vans - Chevrolet & GMC,** V8 & in-line 6 cylinder models '68 thru '92

CHRYSLER

*2058   **Full-size Front-Wheel Drive** '88 thru '93
  K-Cars - see *DODGE Aries* (723)
  Laser - see *DODGE Daytona* (1140)
*1337   **Chrysler & Plymouth Mid-size** front wheel drive '82 thru '93

DATSUN

402   **200SX** all models '77 thru '79
647   **200SX** all models '80 thru '83
228   **B - 210** all models '73 thru '78
525   **210** all models '78 thru '82
206   **240Z, 260Z & 280Z** Coupe '70 thru '78
563   **280ZX** Coupe & 2+2 '79 thru '83
  300ZX - see *NISSAN* (1137)
679   **310** all models '78 thru '82
123   **510 & PL521 Pick-up** '68 thru '73
430   **510** all models '78 thru '81
372   **610** all models '72 thru '76
277   **620 Series Pick-up** all models '73 thru '79
  720 Series Pick-up - see *NISSAN* (771)
376   **810/Maxima** all gasoline models, '77 thru '84
368   **F10** all models '76 thru '79
  Pulsar - see *NISSAN* (876)
  Sentra - see *NISSAN* (982)
  Stanza - see *NISSAN* (981)

DODGE

  400 & 600 - see *CHRYSLER Mid-size* (1337)
*723   **Aries & Plymouth Reliant** '81 thru '89
*1231   **Caravan & Plymouth Voyager Mini-Vans** all models '84 thru '93
699   **Challenger & Plymouth Saporro** all models '78 thru '83
  Challenger '67-'76 - see *DODGE Dart* (234)
236   **Colt** all models '71 thru '77
610   **Colt & Plymouth Champ (front wheel drive)** all models '78 thru '87
*1668   **Dakota Pick-ups** all models '87 thru '93
234   **Dart, Challenger/Plymouth Barracuda & Valiant** 6 cyl models '67 thru '76
*1140   **Daytona & Chrysler Laser** '84 thru '89
*545   **Omni & Plymouth Horizon** '78 thru '90
*912   **Pick-ups** all full-size models '74 thru '91
*556   **Ram 50/D50 Pick-ups & Raider and Plymouth Arrow Pick-ups** '79 thru '91
*1726   **Shadow & Plymouth Sundance** '87 thru '93
*1779   **Spirit & Plymouth Acclaim** '89 thru '92
*349   **Vans - Dodge & Plymouth** V8 & 6 cyl models '71 thru '91

EAGLE

  Talon - see *Mitsubishi Eclipse* (2097)

FIAT

094   **124 Sport Coupe & Spider** '68 thru '78
273   **X1/9** all models '74 thru '80

FORD

*1476   **Aerostar Mini-vans** all models '86 thru '92
788   **Bronco and Pick-ups** '73 thru '79
*880   **Bronco and Pick-ups** '80 thru '91
268   **Courier Pick-up** all models '72 thru '82
1763   **Ford Engine Overhaul Manual**
789   **Escort/Mercury Lynx** all models '81 thru '90
*2046   **Escort/Mercury Tracer** '91 thru '93
*2021   **Explorer & Mazda Navajo** '91 thru '92
560   **Fairmont & Mercury Zephyr** '78 thru '83
334   **Fiesta** all models '77 thru '80
754   **Ford & Mercury Full-size,** Ford LTD & Mercury Marquis ('75 thru '82); Ford Custom 500, Country Squire, Crown Victoria & Mercury Colony Park ('75 thru '87); Ford LTD Crown Victoria & Mercury Gran Marquis ('83 thru '87)
359   **Granada & Mercury Monarch** all in-line, 6 cyl & V8 models '75 thru '80
773   **Ford & Mercury Mid-size,** Ford Thunderbird & Mercury Cougar ('75 thru '82); Ford LTD & Mercury Marquis ('83 thru '86); Ford Torino, Gran Torino, Elite, Ranchero pick-up, LTD II, Mercury Montego, Comet, XR-7 & Lincoln Versailles ('75 thru '86)
*654   **Mustang & Mercury Capri** all models including Turbo. Mustang, '79 thru '92; Capri, '79 thru '86
357   **Mustang V8** all models '64-1/2 thru '73
231   **Mustang II** 4 cyl, V6 & V8 models '74 thru '78
649   **Pinto & Mercury Bobcat** '75 thru '80
1670   **Probe** all models '89 thru '92
*1026   **Ranger/Bronco II** gasoline models '83 thru '93
*1421   **Taurus & Mercury Sable** '86 thru '92
*1418   **Tempo & Mercury Topaz** all gasoline models '84 thru '93
1338   **Thunderbird/Mercury Cougar** '83 thru '88
*1725   **Thunderbird/Mercury Cougar** '89 and '90
*344   **Vans** all V8 Econoline models '69 thru '91

GENERAL MOTORS

*829   **Buick Century, Chevrolet Celebrity, Oldsmobile Cutlass Ciera & Pontiac 6000** all models '82 thru '93
*766   **Buick Skyhawk, Cadillac Cimarron, Chevrolet Cavalier, Oldsmobile Firenza & Pontiac J-2000 & Sunbird** all models '82 thru '92
1420   **Buick Skylark & Somerset, Oldsmobile Calais & Pontiac Grand Am** all models '85 thru '91
*1671   **Buick Regal, Chevrolet Lumina, Oldsmobile Cutlass Supreme & Pontiac Grand Prix** all front wheel drive models '88 thru '90
*2035   **Chevrolet Lumina APV, Oldsmobile Silhouette & Pontiac Trans Sport** all models '90 thru '92

GEO

  Metro - see *CHEVROLET Sprint* (1727)
  Prizm - see *CHEVROLET Nova* (1642)
*2039   **Storm** all models '90 thru '93
  Tracker - see *SUZUKI Samurai* (1626)

GMC

  Safari - see *CHEVROLET ASTRO* (1477)
  Vans & Pick-ups - see *CHEVROLET* (420, 831, 345, 1664)

(Continued on other side)

---

* Listings shown with an asterisk (*) indicate model coverage as of this printing. These titles will be periodically updated to include later model years - consult your Haynes dealer for more information.

Haynes North America, Inc., 861 Lawrence Drive, Newbury Park, CA 91320 • (805) 498-6703

HAYNES AUTOMOTIVE MANUALS

NOTE: New manuals are added to this list on a periodic basis. If you do not see a listing for your vehicle, consult your local Haynes dealer for the latest product information.

HONDA

351	**Accord CVCC** all models '76 thru '83
1221	**Accord** all models '84 thru '89
2067	**Accord** all models '90 thru '93
160	**Civic 1200** all models '73 thru '79
633	**Civic 1300 & 1500 CVCC** '80 thru '83
297	**Civic 1500 CVCC** all models '75 thru '79
1227	**Civic** all models '84 thru '91
*601	**Prelude CVCC** all models '79 thru '89

HYUNDAI

*1552	**Excel** all models '86 thru '93

ISUZU

*1641	**Trooper & Pick-up,** all gasoline models Pick-up, '81 thru '93; Trooper, '84 thru '91

JAGUAR

*242	**XJ6** all 6 cyl models '68 thru '86
*478	**XJ12 & XJS** all 12 cyl models '72 thru '85

JEEP

*1553	**Cherokee, Comanche & Wagoneer Limited** all models '84 thru '93
412	**CJ** all models '49 thru '86
*1777	**Wrangler** all models '87 thru '92

LADA

*413	**1200, 1300. 1500 & 1600** all models including Riva '74 thru '91

MAZDA

648	**626** Sedan & Coupe (rear wheel drive) all models '79 thru '82
*1082	**626 & MX-6** (front wheel drive) all models '83 thru '91
267	**B Series Pick-ups** '72 thru '93
370	**GLC Hatchback** (rear wheel drive) all models '77 thru '83
757	**GLC** (front wheel drive) '81 thru '85
*2047	**MPV** all models '89 thru '93
460	**RX-7** all models '79 thru '85
*1419	**RX-7** all models '86 thru '91

MERCEDES-BENZ

*1643	**190 Series** all four-cylinder gasoline models, '84 thru '88
346	**230, 250 & 280** Sedan, Coupe & Roadster all 6 cyl sohc models '68 thru '72
983	**280 123 Series** gasoline models '77 thru '81
698	**350 & 450** Sedan, Coupe & Roadster all models '71 thru '80
697	**Diesel 123 Series** 200D, 220D, 240D, 240TD, 300D, 300CD, 300TD, 4- & 5-cyl incl. Turbo '76 thru '85

MERCURY

See FORD Listing

MG

111	**MGB** Roadster & GT Coupe all models '62 thru '80
265	**MG Midget & Austin Healey Sprite** Roadster '58 thru '80

MITSUBISHI

*1669	**Cordia, Tredia, Galant, Precis & Mirage** '83 thru '93
*2022	**Pick-up & Montero** '83 thru '93
*2097	**Eclipse, Eagle Talon & Plymouth Laser** '90 thru '94

MORRIS

074	**(Austin) Marina 1.8** all models '71 thru '78
024	**Minor 1000** sedan & wagon '56 thru '71

NISSAN

1137	**300ZX** all models including Turbo '84 thru '89
*1341	**Maxima** all models '85 thru '91
*771	**Pick-ups/Pathfinder** gas models '80 thru '93
876	**Pulsar** all models '83 thru '86
*982	**Sentra** all models '82 thru '90
*981	**Stanza** all models '82 thru '90

OLDSMOBILE

	Bravada - *see CHEVROLET S-10 (831)*
	Calais - *see GENERAL MOTORS (1420)*
	Custom Cruiser - *see BUICK Full-size RWD (1551)*
*658	**Cutlass** all standard gasoline V6 & V8 models '74 thru '88
	Cutlass Ciera - *see GENERAL MOTORS (829)*
	Cutlass Supreme - *see GM (1671)*
	Delta 88 - *see BUICK Full-size RWD (1551)*
	Delta 88 Brougham - *see BUICK Full-size FWD (1551), RWD (1627)*
	Delta 88 Royale - *see BUICK Full-size RWD (1551)*
	Firenza - *see GENERAL MOTORS (766)*
	Ninety-eight Regency - *see BUICK Full-size RWD (1551), FWD (1627)*
	Ninety-eight Regency Brougham - *see BUICK Full-size RWD (1551)*
	Omega - *see PONTIAC Phoenix (551)*
	Silhouette - *see GENERAL MOTORS (2035)*

PEUGEOT

663	**504** all diesel models '74 thru '83

PLYMOUTH

Laser - *see MITSUBISHI Eclipse (2097)*
For other PLYMOUTH titles, see DODGE listing.

PONTIAC

	T1000 - *see CHEVROLET Chevette (449)*
	J-2000 - *see GENERAL MOTORS (766)*
	6000 - *see GENERAL MOTORS (829)*
	Bonneville - *see Buick Full-size FWD (1627), RWD (1551)*
	Bonneville Brougham - *see Buick Full-size (1551)*
	Catalina - *see Buick Full-size (1551)*
1232	**Fiero** all models '84 thru '88
555	**Firebird** V8 models except Turbo '70 thru '81
867	**Firebird** all models '82 thru '92
	Full-size Rear Wheel Drive - *see BUICK Oldsmobile, Pontiac Full-size RWD (1551)*
	Full-size Front Wheel Drive - *see BUICK Oldsmobile, Pontiac Full-size FWD (1627)*
	Grand Am - *see GENERAL MOTORS (1420)*
	Grand Prix - *see GENERAL MOTORS (1671)*
	Grandville - *see BUICK Full-size (1551)*
	Parisienne - *see BUICK Full-size (1551)*
551	**Phoenix & Oldsmobile Omega** all X-car models '80 thru '84
	Sunbird - *see GENERAL MOTORS (766)*
	Trans Sport - *see GENERAL MOTORS (2035)*

PORSCHE

*264	**911** all Coupe & Targa models except Turbo & Carrera 4 '65 thru '89
239	**914** all 4 cyl models '69 thru '76
397	**924** all models including Turbo '76 thru '82
*1027	**944** all models including Turbo '83 thru '89

RENAULT

141	**5 Le Car** all models '76 thru '83
079	**8 & 10** 58.4 cu in engines '62 thru '72
097	**12** Saloon & Estate 1289 cc engine '70 thru '80
768	**15 & 17** all models '73 thru '79
081	**16** 89.7 cu in & 95.5 cu in engines '65 thru '72
	Alliance & Encore - *see AMC (934)*

SAAB

247	**99** all models including Turbo '69 thru '80
*980	**900** all models including Turbo '79 thru '88

SUBARU

237	**1100, 1300, 1400 & 1600** '71 thru '79
*681	**1600 & 1800** 2WD & 4WD '80 thru '89

SUZUKI

*1626	**Samurai/Sidekick and Geo Tracker** all models '86 thru '93

TOYOTA

1023	**Camry** all models '83 thru '91
150	**Carina** Sedan all models '71 thru '74
935	**Celica Rear Wheel Drive** '71 thru '85
*2038	**Celica Front Wheel Drive** '86 thru '92
1139	**Celica Supra** all models '79 thru '92
361	**Corolla** all models '75 thru '79
961	**Corolla** all rear wheel drive models '80 thru '87
*1025	**Corolla** all front wheel drive models '84 thru '92
636	**Corolla Tercel** all models '80 thru '82
360	**Corona** all models '74 thru '82
532	**Cressida** all models '78 thru '82
313	**Land Cruiser** all models '68 thru '82
200	**MK II** all 6 cyl models '72 thru '76
*1339	**MR2** all models '85 thru '87
304	**Pick-up** all models '69 thru '78
*656	**Pick-up** all models '79 thru '92
*2048	**Previa** all models '91 thru '93

TRIUMPH

112	**GT6 & Vitesse** all models '62 thru '74
113	**Spitfire** all models '62 thru '81
322	**TR7** all models '75 thru '81

VW

159	**Beetle & Karmann Ghia** all models '54 thru '79
238	**Dasher** all gasoline models '74 thru '81
*884	**Rabbit, Jetta, Scirocco, & Pick-up** gas models '74 thru '91 & Convertible '80 thru '92
451	**Rabbit, Jetta & Pick-up** all diesel models '77 thru '84
082	**Transporter 1600** all models '68 thru '79
226	**Transporter 1700, 1800 & 2000** all models '72 thru '79
084	**Type 3 1500 & 1600** all models '63 thru '73
1029	**Vanagon** all air-cooled models '80 thru '83

VOLVO

203	**120, 130 Series & 1800 Sports** '61 thru '73
129	**140 Series** all models '66 thru '74
*270	**240 Series** all models '74 thru '90
400	**260 Series** all models '75 thru '82
*1550	**740 & 760 Series** all models '82 thru '88

SPECIAL MANUALS

1479	**Automotive Body Repair & Painting Manual**
1654	**Automotive Electrical Manual**
1667	**Automotive Emissions Control Manual**
1480	**Automotive Heating & Air Conditioning Manual**
1762	**Chevrolet Engine Overhaul Manual**
1736	**GM and Ford Diesel Engine Repair Manual**
1763	**Ford Engine Overhaul Manual**
482	**Fuel Injection Manual**
2069	**Holley Carburetor Manual**
1666	**Small Engine Repair Manual**
299	**SU Carburetors** thru '88
393	**Weber Carburetors** thru '79
300	**Zenith/Stromberg CD Carburetors** thru '76

---

* Listings shown with an asterisk (*) indicate model coverage as of this printing. These titles will be periodically updated to include later model years - consult your Haynes dealer for more information.

Over 100 Haynes motorcycle manuals also available

5-94

Haynes North America, Inc., 861 Lawrence Drive, Newbury Park, CA 91320 • (805) 498-6703